HOLY LIVING

The Christian Tradition for Today

Rowan Williams

BLOOMSBURY
LONDON · OXFORD · NEW YORK · NEW DELHI · SYDNEY

Bloomsbury Continuum
An imprint of Bloomsbury Publishing Plc

50 Bedford Square
London
WC1B 3DP
UK

1385 Broadway
New York
NY 10018
USA

www.bloomsbury.com

Bloomsbury, Continuum and the Diana logo are trademarks of
Bloomsbury Publishing Plc

First published 2017

© Rowan Williams, 2017

Rowan Williams has asserted his right under the Copyright, Designs and
Patents Act, 1988, to be identified as Author of this work.

All rights reserved. No part of this publication may be reproduced or
transmitted in any form or by any means, electronic or mechanical, including
photocopying, recording, or any information storage or retrieval system,
without prior permission in writing from the publishers.

No responsibility for loss caused to any individual or organization acting on
or refraining from action as a result of the material in this publication can be
accepted by Bloomsbury or the author.

British Library Cataloguing-in-Publication Data
A catalogue record for this book is available from the British Library.

Library of Congress Cataloguing-in-Publication data has been applied for.

ISBN: HB: 978-1-4729-4844-1
TPB: 978-1-4729-4608-9
ePDF: 978-1-4729-4609-6
ePub: 978-1-4729-4611-9

2 4 6 8 10 9 7 5 3 1

Typeset by Integra Software Services Pvt. Ltd.
Printed and bound in Great Britain by CPI Group (UK) Ltd, Croydon CR0 4YY

MIX
Paper from
responsible sources
FSC® C020471

To find out more about our authors and books visit www.bloomsbury.com.
Here you will find extracts, author interviews, details of forthcoming events
and the option to sign up for our newsletters.

CONTENTS

CONTENTS

INTRODUCTION

You come out of a memorably good production of a play or a memorably good programme of music, and you talk about it with the people you are with. Did you notice how she handled that moment in the second movement? What about the way he repeated the last line of the last verse? Did you hear his voice rising on that line? Wasn't the break in her voice powerful in the last scene? You're not an actor or a singer or an instrumentalist, and neither are your friends and family; perhaps at best you know you'd like to be able, in an ideal world, to do something like that. But you all have – in different degrees of articulacy – some sense of 'how it works', and an eagerness to explore the mystery and understand it better. You want to get a slightly better grasp of why these moments affect you, change you, open up new possibilities of living in the world.

The only excuse for writing about holiness or about holy lives is something to do with all this. It's a way of pointing to those lives in which something 'works', some wholeness comes through; lives that come across like a brilliant performance of the music or drama of God's action. It helps to notice and think about this or that detail, this or that transition, even as you recognise how far you are from realising it yourself. And as with talking about the play or the concert, what matters finally is the text or the music – not the performers as things in themselves. You have come away with an

enhanced joy in the whole composition, and your appetite is whetted for the next (and probably very different)
performance. So, too, the holy life kindles your engagement with the work itself, the divine action unfolding in
the world, and you become a little better at spotting the
signs of another great performance. And – much more
than in the conversation outside the theatre – you set
your teeth and hope that the reality the story or picture
of a holy life points you to will sink in rather deeper and
make a difference in you.

Great performances point us to the integrity, joy and
demandingness of the whole work. Holy lives point us
to the scope and beauty of God's action. And writing
or talking about holy lives points to the reality of God
coming alive in human words and human bodies. People
who write and talk about these things are quite often,
like the writer of these words, a very long way indeed
from that fullness of life; but they are persuaded that it's
worth trying to point: to invite others to be made fearful
and joyful that the possibilities of faith are made actual,
that the work is indeed performable.

These essays range in style and subject, from general
reflections on what it might mean to live more consciously
and prayerfully in God's presence in and as our bodies,
or on what is and isn't involved in trying to 'know
ourselves', through to more specific studies of particular
holy figures, their teaching and example: Benedict advis-
ing his sixth-century community; Julian of Norwich
blithely turning a set of theological assumptions inside
out to underline more completely the newness of God's
revelation in Jesus; Teresa of Avila exploring how the
Bible makes sense of the lives of herself and her sisters,
and how the Eucharist makes sense of the God whose

work and nature they try to communicate in their daily life. They are essays about how we seek to live honestly and consistently in a community whose purpose is to be 'sacramental', to show the embodied effect of God's gift to humanity in Jesus, and how we seek to be just as honestly and consistently *listeners*, quiet enough to learn how to tune in to what God wants us to hear in the words of the Bible. They span several decades of attempting to point to those places where the Gospel becomes credible, in lives disturbed and healed by God so that they let the light of Jesus Christ come through. Writer and reader may well feel like the group walking away from the theatre: I long to live with that integrity, and I can see just enough of how it comes to be to make me want to understand more. I hope, quite simply, that pointing to these ideas and these lives and teachings will help to open hearts to the depth of judging and trans-forming joy that the drama and music of God's act sets before us.

Rowan Williams

Cambridge, Lent 2017

PART ONE

THE WAY IN

1

TO GIVE AND NOT TO COUNT THE COST

Who is weak and I do not feel weak?

2 Cor. 11.29

Can you drink the cup I drink?

Mk. 10.38

Christ is killed every day by the injuries that we cannot bear. He has borne our griefs and carried our sorrows and our first emotion, our first reaction is relief. Christ who lifts responsibility from us, Christ who suffers for us, Christ who takes away our burden and our misery, who stands between us and the world's dreadfulness, between us and the squalor of our lives, as he was once thought to stand between us and the wrath of his Father. Christ the substitute, Christ the surrogate, Christ who saves us the trouble of being crucified. God will forgive: that is his job; Christ will suffer: that is his. That great and highly uncomfortable saint, Raymond Raynes, once described the aim of most Western European religion as being, 'to shut up sacrifice in Jesus alone and not let it pass to us'. 'Can you drink the cup I drink or be baptized with the baptism I am baptized with?' Less passionate than James or John – or more honest – we answer, 'No. No, Lord, your cup is yours alone; far be it from us to presume to share it'. By the grace of God we know our limitations.

And so Christ is killed every day by the injuries we refuse, by what we will not let ourselves feel and know, by the risks we refuse, the involvement we refuse. The Gospel tells us of some who knew their limitations: a rich young man, a dutiful son who returned to bury his father, a secret disciple who emerged to bury Jesus himself, the nameless followers who walked no more with him, two clergymen on the road to Jericho, and a man by the name of Judas Iscariot, the son of Simon. No, not one of them is condemned; they are rational men who have taken the Lord's advice and counted the cost. They know more about discipleship than the eager hearers of the Word who press forward to offer their services with adolescent enthusiasm. To such, as to James and John, Jesus addresses those flat and bitter words, 'You don't know what you are asking'.

Yet it is the realists who are the murderers of Christ. It is the Grand Inquisitor who has calculated the cost of discipleship to the full, who has taken every step towards Christ except the last: it is he who is the greatest enemy of Christ. Behind Pilate stands the compassionate and far-sighted Caiaphas; behind Caiaphas stands Judas; behind Judas, the rich young ruler. The midnight session of the council that sent Jesus to his death is the great conspiracy of reasonable people in every age, of people who know their limitations. Jesus in Gethsemane is left alone and unsupported in his tortured prayer, because the apostles – who once perhaps thought they understood – have decided that they cannot go with him into that desert and sensibly have gone to sleep. *Agape* – in the older translation – 'bears all things' (2 Cor. 13.7) and bears them alone. 'I looked, but there was no one to help' (Is. 63.5). For the reasonable person, in the humility

8

of their realism, declines the bloody and compromising struggle.

Well, we are all realists to a greater or lesser degree, and there is therefore no avoiding the fact of our complicity in the death of Jesus. Like the apostles we evade and refuse and deny and escape when the cross becomes a serious possibility. Terror of involvement, fear of failure – of hurting as well as being hurt – the dread of having our powerlessness nakedly spelled out for us: all this is the common coin of most of our lives. For beneath the humility of the person who believes he or she knows their limitations is the fear of those who have never found or felt their limitations. Only when we have travelled to those stony places of the spirit where we are forced to confront our helplessness and our failure can we be said to know our limitations, and then the knowledge is too late to be useful. We do not know what we can or cannot bear until we have risked the impossible and intolerable in our own lives. Christ bears what is unbearable, but we must first find it and know it to be unbearable. And it does not stop being ours when it becomes his. Only thus can we translate our *complicity* in the death of Christ into a *communion* in the death of Christ, a baptism into the death of Christ: by not refusing, by not escaping, by forgetting our realism and our reasonableness, by letting the heart speak freely, by exposing ourselves, by making ourselves vulnerable.

Living in community – in a college, or a marriage, or a monastery – we are daily confronted with the invitation to involvement at one level or another. And every community furnishes a rich variety of the techniques of evasion. Every community sees to it that protective devices are available from the slot machine, that the paths of retreat are fully signposted. After all, we do not want to impose, we do not want to pry, we do not want to interfere. Let everyone work out their salvation in fear and trembling. Now God forbid that we should cultivate a morbid curiosity concerning the state of our neighbour's soul, or that we should strive to reduce our relationships to that state commonly associated with the therapy group or with the public bar at five to eleven on a Saturday evening. No, these too are the mechanisms of illusion. Involvement may be a less dramatic, if not less costly, matter, of learning to listen: to listen to the silence in the voices of others, to watch the spaces in their actions. To attend to them in self-forgetfulness, as one attends to a complex and concentrated task, to a piece of music, to the performance of a ritual, to meditation: so that we hardly notice what it is we are being drawn into until, perhaps, we reach those much vaunted limitations of ours, the thresholds of our pain. And here we shall find that there is no going back, no unravelling the thread, only a holding to the foot of the cross which we have discovered. What we shall feel, what we shall know, is determined only by the needs of our neighbour – once we have taken the costly first step of refusing to be reasonable, refusing to predict and calculate, refusing above all to make policies about our response to people.

We hear a great deal about the need for detachment or 'professionalism' in the life of the priest. Humanly speaking, of course, we are not going to enter into deep intimacies with everyone we encounter, and it is romantic silliness to pretend that we are. There is an authentic realism, born of the irony of authentic humility. But if 'detachment' and 'professionalism' mean any more than, on the one hand, the recognition of this fact, and on the other, the confession that our individual resources will have to yield at some unknown point to the hiddenness of Christ's work – if they mean any more than this – they are the enemies of the Gospel and the tools of the Grand Inquisitor. Paul's fierce and passionate involvement with the lives of his Corinthian converts knows nothing of detachment in the cheap and facile sense in which it is so regularly used: 'Who is weak and I do not feel weak? Who is led into sin, and I do not inwardly burn?' (2 Cor. 11.29). And he was later to speak, with a boldness that is still deeply shocking, of filling up 'what is still lacking in regard to Christ's afflictions' (Col. 1.24). The complete involvement of Jesus in human torment draws us after, draws us to imitation, stirs us to be Christ for our neighbour, to expose ourselves as he did.

And yet we cannot. There is an ultimate costliness which, of ourselves, we cannot bear. At the end of our involvement the poverty and inadequacy of our compassion is brutally and nakedly shown us; there and there only can we meet the Christ who accepts and transfigures our poverty. There we can see with something like clarity the radical depths of compassion and involvement; what it means to say that Jesus has borne our griefs and carried our sorrows; what it costs God to redeem us by taking our pain into himself. There we may begin to understand that the pain of the world is of a seriousness that can be met only by and in the life of God; and that our discipleship, our involvement, is only possible because this life is made ours. Without it, there is only despair, a despair which paralyses action and dries up compassion. It promises us neither protection nor consolation, but only *grace*, the free privilege of carrying the cross of Christ and being upheld in his arms through every darkness and torture, so that the weight of the cross does not crush us. This is the heart of the apostolate – 'Struck down but not destroyed. We always carry around in our body the death of Jesus, so that the life of Jesus may also be revealed in our mortal body' (2 Cor. 4.10).

Christian life, Christian ministry, is not a matter of calculation or of realism. Risk is incalculable, grace is incalculable, Christ is incalculable. He calls us to abandon policy and protectiveness, to attend to and respond to his Word sounding in all human hurt, to be wounded and find out our helplessness – and there to meet the absolute gratuity and unexpectedness of his measureless compassion. But he will not wipe the tears from our eyes until we have learned to weep.

2

HEALTH AND HEALING

*When an impure spirit comes out of a person, it goes
through arid places seeking rest and does not find it.
Then it says, 'I will return to the house I left'. When
it arrives, it finds the house unoccupied, swept clean
and put in order. Then it goes and takes with it seven
other spirits more wicked than itself, and they go in
and live there. And the final condition of that person
is worse than the first.*

Matt. 12.43–5

One of Jesus's most powerful and memorable images
is this picture of the self as an untenanted space, an
uninhabited space into which flow the forces of destruction. I want to suggest that our theology of health and
healing is connected with understanding how the world
comes to be 'inhabited'. You'll be familiar with the
way in which St Paul, in more than one letter, speaks
about the 'flesh', the system of destructive reactions and
instincts that keeps us prisoner to sin. In his catalogue
in Galatians 5 of the 'works of the flesh', he begins
with the more obvious kinds of physical transgression
or disorder – debauchery, sexual immorality, idolatry,
witchcraft – and then goes on to a number of things
that don't seem so clearly related to the physical –

ambition, party spirit, envy and so forth – before return-ing firmly to the physical realm with drunkenness and orgies. In the light of this, it's clear that the flesh, as St Paul uses the term, is a word that describes human life lived in an assortment of dysfunctional relations – manipulative, self-serving, self-aggrandising; a situation in which the human self is experienced as an empty space to be filled by gratification secured by power.

In fact we can read St Paul as filling out what Jesus says. What he is describing is an untenanted, uninhab-ited human life: 'flesh' is human life that is not properly inhabited, human life somehow alienated, cut off from its environment, cut off from that life of 'spirit' which in St Paul's usage is always about life-giving relatedness. And if salvation in its widest sense is understood as the bringing together of flesh and spirit in *body*, then perhaps we can see how all this has some pertinence to what we mean by health. Remember that the gift of the Spirit in St Paul's theology is always a gift that creates relatedness; which is why the life of the human spirit, as opposed to the life of the flesh, is life in free relation to God and generous relation to one another. Flesh is the opposite of this, a system of empty, untenanted life, where there is no spark to kindle in relation. So the process of our salva-tion can be described as the story of how 'flesh' becomes something fuller, becomes body, ultimately as part of the body of Christ, a temple of God's Holy Spirit. And the Bible assumes, from beginning to end, that this mate-rial flesh, the dust and clay of the Genesis narrative, is made to be inhabited, and indeed that the entire material world is made to be inhabited by the action of God.

God's grace makes people fully human. And if what I've said so far makes sense then we can understand this as meaning that God's grace typically makes flesh to be inhabited by spirit, just as in the creation story God breathes into the dust and clay he has shaped so that this passive stuff becomes 'a living being' (Gen. 2.7). Flesh is made to be something more than a dead lump of untenanted material which lies around for other people to fall over. It becomes a life and thus a language, a system, a means of connection. As we shall see, this is not just something that is pertinent to the theology of health, as if that were simply one isolated part of the map; it opens up an insight into theology as a whole. We are able to read the whole of the theological enterprise as tracing how God transforms flesh; how, at all sorts of different levels, God makes flesh inhabited by creating living relationship with himself. There is a surface awkwardness about these words, of course, in that when we speak of flesh being inhabited we can easily run away with the idea that 'something' is being injected into this lump of flesh from outside. But what the Bible seems to assume is a somewhat different picture, in which the life of the body, the animated and communicating flesh, is a flowering of what is already given, not the importation of some 'extra'.

To say that theology is the art of tracing how God transforms the flesh by creating living relationship with God, and by this means creating living relationship with the rest of what God has made, is to say that every good and positive human story is about how flesh comes to be inhabited, how flesh is filled with meaning. How do we tell the story of our own lives? Not simply as a record of what happened to this particular lump of fat and bone. We can tell our story as a story of how we learned to speak and to relate, to respond and to interact – how we came to live, to inhabit this fleshly place with all the energies God gives. A novel about the growth of a human self is a characteristic way in which, in Western culture, we tell such a story – a *Bildungsroman*, as the Germans call it, chronicling the evolution of the sense of self emerging in the place where we happen to live, our given relationships becoming connections we own and understand and consciously nourish. A good love story is supremely a story about how flesh comes to be inhabited and comes to mean what had never been dreamed of.

And so for the theologian, the story being told is about how flesh comes to signify the greatest and most comprehensive meaning of all, how it comes to 'mean' God himself – how flesh is so inhabited by the life of God that, in relation to God, it becomes transfigured and transfiguring. 'The Word became flesh and made his dwelling among us,' says the fourth Gospel (Jn. 1.14). God lives his life in a human identity, filling flesh with the divine communication and the divine freedom itself. This most fully 'inhabited', most fully 'saturated' flesh which is the humanity of Jesus Christ becomes the supreme instance of health, flesh and spirit in one body that proves to be incapable of destruction because it is so intensely related, with such life-giving completeness, to both creator and creation. The presence of God's Word, God's freedom to love and to communicate, so permeates that piece of the human world which is Jesus of Nazareth that the fullest possible meanings of God are communicated there and the very freedom of God is acted out in that life to make us free. Christ's body is an instrument of grace, as a Church of England report on the healing ministry put it some years ago.

So the story which theology tells and theology reflects on is the most comprehensive version of a story we're telling ourselves and one another all the time: our own stories of how our flesh came to mean something, came to say something. We can tell it in terms simply of what brought us to be who we are here and now; we can tell it more specifically in terms of a love story – and sometimes, too, a tragic story of the loss of love or relation. We can tell it sometimes in the context of a therapeutic relationship, allowing a practised listener to draw it out further. We can tell it in the medium of artistic creation. And as the story unfolds, the world is shown not to be an empty space, and we see how our 'fleshly' identity is suffused by spirit and becomes a tenanted place.

(There have been some very significant studies in recent years of Asperger's Syndrome, particularly the series of monographs from various authors published by Jessica Kingsley – studies of the various therapeutic means that are developing of making connections with adults and children who live with this condition. What seems to happen when such work succeeds is an enabling of communication through attending to the rhythms and patterns of bodily behaviour, and learning to 'read' these patterns as communication in their own terms; to echo and feed back, and so to make plain that this space is indeed 'inhabited' and can in some ways be shared, in a relation that isn't always easy to connect to conventional expectations, but is no less a manifestation of flesh becoming body.)

We have already noted the assumption in all this that health is something to do with the bridging of a gulf or healing of a schism between flesh and spirit. Often if we look hard and carefully at the stories of healing in the

Gospels, we can read them as describing how healing emerges in a situation where, as we think more closely about it, there is some sort of concealed alienation, some sort of bruised relationship. It is too simple to say only that Jesus heals people who are sick in mind and body and everyone is glad. While that may be the bottom line in these stories, it is clear that the act of healing itself is again and again bound up with the overcoming of various schisms and exclusions, various kinds of isolation or alienation.

In the first four stories of healing in St Mark's Gospel this comes over pretty plainly. There is the dramatic story of the demoniac in the synagogue, who cries out in fear that Jesus has come to destroy. The empty, 'fleshly life' is precisely one that lives in the fear of being destroyed, because of its lack of rootedness in a reality beyond the ego – and in that fear destroys itself more and more deeply, inviting in more destructive forces and colluding with them. Not surprisingly, when fullness appears in the shape of God's Word in flesh, the reaction is terror. Next we have a story about Simon Peter's mother-in-law: not so obvious a case at first sight, but what we are seeing is how relationship with Jesus (Peter's relationship) flows over into a healing relationship with those connected to the people related to Jesus. Relating to Jesus is not something that excludes other relationships, but rather something that brings further life and hope to them. And in the next story, the healing of the leper, we have most painfully obviously an instance of someone whose sickness is profoundly bound up with exclusion, who is not permitted to be part of a worshipping and thanking community. His healing, therefore, is completed by going to show himself to the priest and so to rejoin the life of a community that praises God. And when, in the last of this quartet, the paralytic is let down through the roof by his friends, Jesus's first response is a word of *forgiveness,* recognizing that what is presenting on the surface has something to do with an inner alienation, fear or guilt.

In all these stories and many more, what is happening in Jesus's healings is the restoration or extension of relation, inclusion in community, the bridging of a gulf between spirit and empty or alienated flesh. These people, as they are healed or exorcised, come to be places newly inhabited – by love, by thanksgiving, by peace, by the sense of absolution. That is why healing, in these stories, is more than simply the act that restores physical health where there was physical or mental sickness. Somewhere in the background is a brokenness, an emptiness, that needs to be addressed, and into which Jesus speaks; and the act of healing frees the person to express what they are made and called to be, which is members of a community that lives in gratitude and in praise – members of a community in which flesh gives voice to spirit and, in so doing, creates further networks of healing, integrating relation.

There are two other stories that give some extra perspective on this. One is St Luke's story (Lk. 17.11–19) of the ten lepers who were healed, and the one who returns to give thanks. He is told that his faith has made him well because *the act of thanksgiving is the end of the story of healing.* The healed person is again part of a community which gives thanks and utters praise, which celebrates and which therefore fulfils what human beings are made to be. The other, rather darker, story, is the one which appears after the narrative of the

19

Transfiguration in the Synoptic Gospels: the man with an epileptic son who waits at the foot of the mountain while the disciples try, without success, to cast out the demon, a demon which, says the father, casts the boy into 'fire and water', as if the inner emptiness of diabolical action becomes also a kind of anger with the body. It is this deep rupture of angry refusal of the body which Jesus's healing has to address.

These stories offer some of the principles on which we can proceed to think through a little further not only what a theology of health is about but also, as I have already hinted, what *theology itself* is about. This vision of health as the reconciliation of flesh and spirit in body, the making of flesh to be inhabited by spirit in life-giving relationship with God and others – this account of health can take us in two directions in our thinking about healing. Of course it is impossible to ignore the physicality of the healing described in the Gospels: there is no way around that, nor should there be. Jesus did actually make sick people better in a perfectly simple and straightforward sense, according to the Gospel narratives. We should not get too sophisticated about that: the reconciliation of flesh and spirit in these stories is deeply bound up with restoring the real and bodily freedom of a suffering person to return to that place where they are free *in their flesh* to praise God in community. In these cases, this involves being made whole in a simple, physical sense.

But as we understand this theologically we also see the possibility of understanding healing more fully. Reconciliation with the body can take many forms; it is not necessarily evasive or rationalistic to say that healing may also be about reconciliation with or in a body that is not going to 'get better' physically in the straightforward sense. There are reconciliations and liberations that will happen within a situation which, physically, may not change much – which is what so many learn through ministry with the terminally ill, or with those who live with long-standing, continuing 'disabilities'. We know that there may be a healing in such circumstances that has to do with a new capacity to inhabit the body, a freedom within a body which may be dying, mortal, limited, afflicted, in all kinds of ways. And what is common to both the more obvious kind of physical healing and this kind of reconciliation with where the suffering body is, is surely that healing is made real in terms of what makes it possible for an embodied spirit to praise God in community with other embodied spirits. This may equally well be material healing or the renewed sense of how to inhabit a body which is dying, limited and suffering.

I shouldn't want to generalise further; we will be in trouble if we try to say that the only 'real' healing is physical improvement, or the only 'real' healing some sort of inner transformation. Neither of these will do, and neither of them does justice to how the New Testament relates stories of healing: never *just* the solution of a physical problem, never just the expulsion of a hostile power without the addressing of bruised, limited or damaged relationship and the reclaiming of what could be a dangerously empty space. This is how the imagery of healing becomes so central to the whole business of how we grow and develop and become holy (a word clearly related in so many languages to health and healing) as embodied persons.

Sin, as St Paul sees it – certainly in Galatians 5, but in many other places too – seems to be very much about uninhabited flesh, our humanity experienced in a mean-ingless, destructive or isolating way. The habits of the 'flesh' which keep us prisoner in our relation with God, that set a ceiling on our growth towards God, are the habits of an empty fleshliness, the opposite of genu-ine bodily presence. Who was it who said (alarmingly) that by the age of 40 you have the face you deserve? A half-serious observation, perhaps, but one that reflects something very serious about how we are with one another – and the difference between inhabited and uninhabited faces. W. H. Auden's little epigram about how 'private faces in public places' are 'wiser and nicer' than 'public faces in private places' is another version of this. It's often worth asking, when we are struggling in an encounter with another person, whether we are seeing in them an 'inhabited' face, 'private' in the sense that it is capable of looking inward. And those of us who habitually have to speak in public may very well ask ourselves awkward questions about this. Faces may appear 'uninhabited' because a person is living or work-ing at a level that is unhelpfully protected, unhelpfully resistant to scrutiny, external or internal. We learn a great deal simply from looking at faces. The instinct of the Eastern Orthodox Church that our own holiness is enriched by looking at the faces of the holy – in the flesh or through the icon – is a sound one. When I think of the people I have known in my life who are most obviously holy, what I think of is faces that look – in the best sense – *lived in*.

As I've said, it is not necessarily some kind of evasion to suggest that there is more to a theology of health and healing than simply treating healing as a demonstration of divine power in solving determinate physical or mental problems. This is not how the Gospels tell the story, nor does it sit well with the picture of humanity that the New Testament and, indeed, Scripture as a whole offers us. We are led in all this towards a whole way of looking at theology itself – theology as the art of tracing how God transforms flesh by creating living relationship. Theology, therefore, is a discipline that traces the process of how the world comes to be inhabited. The biblical story itself begins with a picture of a world that is empty, waste and void; and God decides that this void will be inhabited by the breath of his Spirit and the further work of his hands. History begins; the world becomes a system of relatedness and shared meanings. Theology tells how the world in general, human history in particular, and your human body and mine in even further particular, come to be inhabited by the gift of God. And we can speak of healing precisely as the means for this, just as we can speak of repentance or conversion as the means on our side for this to happen, and of the transfiguring work of the Spirit as that which holds it all together. Healing aims at what theology deals with: a spirit-inhabited body, or even a body *becoming* spirit, living in a world in a mode that transfigures that world and reshapes its meaning in and through Jesus Christ. Christ's inhabiting of the world and the body for the sake of healing in the broadest sense has made this possible.

It is not just that God has made a world to be inhabited; God has made a world which *God* purposes to inhabit, and which in some sense God does already inhabit, in the wisdom, the beauty, the order, the alluring wonder that surrounds us in our material environment. God is already inhabiting what has been made; but the task that God undertakes in our human history is the longer and more complex one of inhabiting the thoughts and feelings, the reactions, passions, griefs and exhilarations of contingent and messy human beings like you and me. And the pivotal moment in the unfolding narrative is when God fully and unequivocally inhabits the human life which is Jesus of Nazareth, the death and the resurrection that belong to Jesus of Nazareth, and so makes the unprecedented difference to your body and mine which we call grace and adoption and the life of the Body of Christ, the difference that changes our own inhabiting of the world.

In this light, it is important to link healing in its more narrowly focused sense with everything we want to say about the Gospel. I have been suggesting, in effect, that the good news which the Gospel tells us is, first of all, that the world is inhabited, with increasing intensity and fullness as time goes on, by its maker; second, that the maker of the world has made it possible for *us* to inhabit the world more fully, more deeply and joyfully than we could ever have imagined. And this inhabiting of the world, this reconciliation between flesh and spirit, involves something more than simply healing in the conventional sense; it involves our self-knowledge, our art and our science, our labours for justice: because all of these are about the fully human inhabiting of our environment. A world in which there was no hunger and thirst for justice would be a world of 'flesh' only. We would be looking at our fellow humans as if they were untenanted and abstract spaces in the world. Similarly, a world without art would be a world in which flesh sat on its depressing own, without any passion to discover how the environment is lived in by God's glory and reflected in word and in image.

I have mentioned self-knowledge too in this connection, which may sound a strange thing to bring in here, but is in fact quite an important dimension of this story. The Gospel tells us that we can and must learn to 'inhabit' our own lives and our memories, to come to terms with, be at peace with ourselves, to remember who we are without pain and alienation, because we trust a forgiving God. This too is part of what the Gospel promises in the way of healing, and so of inhabiting our world and our bodies. Above all, this process has to do with the way in which we learn to inhabit world and body in prayer – prayer which is not, in spite of a good deal of encouragement to think otherwise, an activity that goes on outside or in parallel to the body, but is essentially the act of an embodied spirit. Remember the phrase used earlier on, about embodied spirits praising God in community with other embodied spirits: this is where prayer begins and ends. And the way in which we learn to *be our bodies* as we pray, to attend to our bodies and be conscious of how they inform the desire and the openness that prayer seeks – this is something we are slowly learning again in our often somewhat arid modern Western Christian world.

In the perspective of the whole Christian tradition, this is by no means a marginal eccentricity. Teresa of Avila – a 'standard', orthodox Catholic mystic, after all – describes how, at the beginning of your life of prayer, you are mostly aware of *disorientation*. You don't know quite what is going on, and strange things may happen in your body; you may feel that you're not in control of the body, or even that you are 'out' of it. But as you become accustomed to God's indwelling and become more deeply at home with God, prayer is something that happens from the bodily place where you are or *that* you are. Teresa describes her memory of the day when she decided she no longer wanted to be dead, the Feast of St Mary Magdalene in 1571; when she realized that some kind of breakthrough had occurred in her life of prayer which made it possible for her to say that she was content to be with God here and now, to serve and walk with him in this life as long as God wanted. So when she speaks about 'walking with God among the pots and pans' in the kitchen, and recognizes that the vocations of Mary and Martha are not quite as far away as she once thought, she is in effect affirming that it is as *this* body, speaking, moving and acting *here*, that she is praying; her journey has been back to the starting point that is this present moment. The story that theology tells and which a theology of health, in particular, will bring to the fore, is the story of that journey.

This theological perspective helps us ask questions of a view of health that is narrowly functional, and a view of healing that is simply about making things better for individuals. It helps us make those connections I've mentioned with the arts, with therapy, with the labour for justice; and in so doing it puts fruitful questions about how theology itself is to be done. Is our theology a story of healing? Can it be re-imagined as a story about how peace is made between flesh and spirit, a story of how God's inhabiting of the world in creation, redemption and sanctification bridges the gulf which constantly opens up when we're not looking between flesh and spirit? The great Russian theologian Vladimir Lossky famously observed that if you want to know what the face of the Holy Spirit looked like you should look at the faces of the saints. You learn to look at inhabited faces: faces that have stopped being 'flesh' in the negative sense with which we began, untenanted, empty places where relation doesn't happen, the spark doesn't kindle; where there is a deadness of isolation that makes us less than human.

God has made us to live as material beings in a material world and has made us, therefore, as creatures who have to learn how to live in that kind of world. Because we have intelligence and love and imagination, our living in our environment is an evolving story, not just a given fact. The story of our salvation is the story of that learning, taught by the God who brings the very divine life itself to inhabit our world, to touch, to heal, to promise and to transfigure. We need to recover the sense that the Gospel is always about healing, because it is always about telling effectively and transformingly how God has inhabited and continues to inhabit this world. The Gospel tells this in word, image and concept, and we tell it in our theology and our practice, in what we do in our work for justice, in our art, in our care and our pasturing, remembering that one of the greatest paradoxes of the Christian faith is that we only learn to live in 'heaven' – in the presence of our maker, saviour and lover – when we learn to live on earth, here and now inhabiting the space in which God has placed us.

3

The Bible Today: Reading & Hearing

One of the things that most clearly and universally identifies Christians as Christians is that they habitually read the Bible – or have the Bible read to them. From the most liberal to the most conservative, from Pentecostalists in Venezuela to Orthodox in Albania, those who call themselves Christians are engaged in a complex and varied set of relationships with this written text, relationships which shape the patterns of worship, teaching and ethical discourse. Not even the most tradition-bound and hierarchical Christian community has ever seriously argued that the authority of the contemporary hierarchy can wholly displace the reading of Scripture, or that the language of Scripture is anything but finally normative in some sense for the community. And even the most ideologically insistent liberal is unlikely to argue that Scripture can be relegated entirely to the level of illustrative historical material about the remote beginnings of the faith (though the last century has seen a repeated swing in that direction, even if it has never quite got to that point of blunt denial).

In what follows, I don't intend to offer a novel theory of inspiration, or a set of tools that will finally settle the current debates over interpretation within and between the churches; my aim is a very modest one, to examine the practice of reading the Bible so as to tease out some of what it tells us about the nature of Christian identity itself. Because some of our present difficulties are, at the very least, compounded by the collision of theologically inept or rootless accounts of Scripture, and it seems imperative to work at a genuine theology of the Bible as the sacred literature of the Church. Popular appeals to the obvious leave us battling in the dark; and the obvious – not surprisingly – looks radically different to different people. For many, it is obvious that a claim to the effect that Scripture is 'God's Word written' implies a particular set of beliefs about the Bible's inerrancy. For others, it is equally obvious that, if you are not that savage and menacing beast called a 'fundamentalist', you are bound to see the Bible as a text of its time: instructive, even sporadically inspiring, but subject to rethinking in the light of our more advanced position. As I hope will become evident, I regard such positions as examples of the rootlessness that afflicts our use of the Bible; and I hope that these reflections may suggest a few ways of reconnecting with a more serious theological grasp of the Church's relation with Scripture.

To begin with the simplest point: before Scripture is read in private, it is heard in public. Those of us who assume that the normative image of Scripture reading is the solitary individual poring over a bound volume, one of the great icons of classical Protestantism, may need to be reminded that for most Christians throughout the ages and probably most in the world at present, the norm is listening. Very few early or mediaeval Christians could possibly have owned a Bible; not many in the rapidly growing churches of the developing world today are likely to either. And this underlines the fact that the Church's public use of the Bible represents the Church as defined in some important way by listening: the community when it comes together doesn't only break bread and reflect together and intercede, it silences itself to hear something. It represents itself in that moment as a community existing in response to a word of summons or invitation, to an act of communication that requires to be heard and answered.

So the Church in reading Scripture publicly says both that it is not a self-generated reality, created simply out of human reflection and ideals, and that what is read needs to be read as a communicative act – that is, not as information, not as just instruction, but as a summons to assemble together as a certain sort of community, one that understands itself as called and created 'out of nothing'. Whatever we do in private with our reading of Scripture, we must do in awareness of this public character. The Church – a familiar enough point – is in the language of the Bible itself an 'assembly', a 'convocation': an *ekklesia*. It declares its basic character when it represents itself as listening to the act of 'convoking', calling together. From one (crucially important) point of view, the celebration of the Eucharist is that representation, the moment when all are equally and unequivocally designated as guests, responding to invitation. But, since the authoritative and defining patterns of Christian practice never reduce themselves to single and simple models, from another point of view, the hearing of the Bible is that representation. As I hope to suggest later, these two basic ways in which the Church says what it is cast a lot of light on each other.

Now this already implies a certain challenge in understanding the Bible. Not all of it by any means is cast in the grammatical form of invitation or summons. There are substantial bits of it that read like that – much of the Mosaic Law and the Prophets, and the letters of Christian Scripture, for example. But we have to work out what it means to say that a Hebrew genealogy, the Song of Songs, the laments of Job and the Psalmist, the narratives of the Gospels and the visions of Revelation are equally acts of communication whose effect is to convoke the assembly of faithful. It must sometimes strike the worshipper as slightly strange to be asked to say, 'This is the Word of the Lord' at the end of a passage addressed to the Lord – not least one addressed to the Lord in terms of query or even reproach.

Two principles emerge very directly from this, though they are not always stated clearly in the Church. The first is that when we are dealing with texts that are grammatically addressed to a specific audience, we are being asked to imagine that historically remote audience as not only continuous with us but in some sense one with us. Just as in Deuteronomy, there is an insistence that the words spoken at Sinai are being spoken 'not to your forefathers' but to 'us' here present today – to all those in the liturgical assembly at any moment in Israel's history (Deut. 5.2–5), so for the Christian, and the Jewish, believer. We, here and now, are incorporated in the audience. The second principle is that in dealing with texts that are not grammatically directed in this way, we are obliged to ask, 'What does this text suggest or imply about the changes which reading it or hearing it might bring about?' The Bible itself gives us a cardinal example of 'texts' – oral recitations in this case – clearly intended to effect change: the parables of Jesus. And the sort of change they envisage is the result of being forced to identify yourself within the world of the narrative, to recognise who you are or might be, and how your situation is included in what the parable narrates.

These principles need a good deal of further filling out if we are to be able to apply them to some of the hardest interpretative cases, but they are significant and, I'd say, primary implications of the practice of hearing Scripture publicly. Both tell us that the 'time' in which we hear Scripture is not like ordinary time. We are contemporary with events remote in history; we are caught up in the time of recitation, when we are to reimagine ourselves. For this moment, we exist simply as listeners, suspending our questions while the question is put to us of how we are to speak afresh about ourselves. We stand at a point of origin, and, as listeners, our primary responsibility is to receive. Kierkegaard stressed this receptive dimension eloquently in some of his writings; but an excellent discussion by Alan Jacobs[1] points out importantly that there is a risk of so glossing the receptivity of the reader/hearer as to dissolve the proper tension between I and Other. Receiving as itself an act of enabling communication requires the free engagement of a self with skills and history. What this might mean we shall come back to shortly. But it remains true that this level of reading cannot happen if we are dominated by the time we think we occupy, so that anything coming at us through an alien text is likely to be processed into whatever most concerns us now and subjected to the criteria by which we judge something as useful or useless for the time of our plans and projects. And this has some implications for the whole of our thinking about worship, of course.

Among those skills we need to bring for receptivity is a capacity to think through what the initial relation between text and audience might be. I am not thinking primarily here of the way in which good critical scholarship elucidates such relations, though that is one of the underappreciated gifts of intellectual modernity – the enrichment of sheer historical imagination in ways barely accessible to most premodern readers and hearers. What I have in mind is a more basic matter, the capacity to read/hear enough to sense the directedness of a text. Fragmentary reading is highly risky to the extent that it abstracts from what various hermeneutical theorists (Paul Ricoeur above all)[2] have thought of as the world 'in front of the text' – the specific needs that shape the movement and emphasis of the text itself. Elements in that text may be valid and significant, but yet be capable of partial and even distorting use if not seen as part of a rhetorical process or argument. It is always worth asking, 'What is the text as a full unit trying not to say or to deny?'

Two contentious examples. The first of them is, as we shall see, of more than accidental importance in understanding certain things about Scripture as a whole, but I choose it because of its frequent use in modern debates about relations between faith communities. Jesus says in the Farewell Discourses of John's Gospel that 'no-one comes to the Father except by me'. As an isolated text, this is regularly used to insist that salvation depends upon explicit confession of Christ, and therefore as a refutation of any attempt to create a more 'inclusive' theology of interfaith relations. But the words come at the end of a typically dense and compressed piece of exposition. Jesus has, at the end of chapter 13, explained that the disciples cannot follow him now; he goes ahead to prepare a place. Thus, he creates the path to the Father that the disciples must follow; they know the path already in the sense that they know him. And this knowledge of him, expressed in the mutual love that he has made possible (13.34–5), will carry them through the devastation of absence and not-knowing which will follow the crucifixion. Seeing and knowing Jesus as he goes towards his death in the perfection of his 'love for his own' is already in some way a knowing of the Father as that goal towards which the self-giving of Jesus in life and death is directed. The Father is not to be known apart from this knowledge of Jesus.

Now this certainly does not suggest in any direct way a more inclusive approach to other faiths. But the point is that the actual question being asked is not about the fate of non-Christians; it is about how the disciples are to understand the death of Jesus as the necessary clearing of the way which they are to walk. If they are devastated and left desolate by his death, they have not grasped that it is itself the opening of a way which would otherwise remain closed to them. Thus it is part of the theology of the cross that is evolving throughout the later chapters of John, the mapping out of a revelation of glory through self-forgetting and self-offering. The text in question indeed states that there is no way to the Father except by virtue of what Jesus does and suffers; but precisely because that defines the way we must then follow, it is (to say the least) paradoxical if it is used as a simple self-affirmation for the exclusive claim of the Christian institution or the Christian system. There is, in other words, a way of affirming the necessity of Christ's crucified mediation that has the effect of undermining the very way it is supposed to operate. If we ask what the question is that the passage overall poses, or what the change is that needs to be taking place over the time of the passage's narration, it is about the move from desolation in the face of the cross (Jesus's cross and the implicit demand for the disciple to carry the cross also) to confidence that the process is the work of love coming from and leading to the Father.

My second example is even more contentious in the present climate; and once again I must stress that the point I am making is not that the reading I propose settles a controversy or changes a substantive interpretation, but that many current ways of reading miss the actual direction of the passage and so undermine a proper theological approach to Scripture. Paul in the first chapter of Romans famously uses same-sex relationships as an illustration of human depravity – along with other 'unnatural' behaviours such as scandal, disobedience to parents and lack of pity. It is, for the majority of modern readers, the most important single text in Scripture on the subject of homosexuality, and has understandably been the focus of an enormous amount of exegetical attention.

What is Paul's argument? And, once again, what is the movement that the text seeks to facilitate? The answer is in the opening of chapter 2: we have been listing examples of the barefaced perversity of those who cannot see the requirements of the natural order in front of their noses; well, it is precisely the same perversity that affects those who have received the revelation of God and persist in self-seeking and self-deceit. The change envisaged is from confidence in having received divine revelation to an awareness of universal sinfulness and need. Once again, there is a paradox in reading Romans 1 as a foundation for identifying in others a level of sin that is not found in the chosen community.

Now this gives little comfort to either party in the current culture wars in the Church. It is not helpful for a 'liberal' or revisionist case, since the whole point of Paul's rhetorical gambit is that everyone in his imagined readership agrees in thinking the same-sex relations of the culture around them to be as obviously immoral as idol-worship or disobedience to parents. It is not very helpful to the conservative either, though, because Paul insists on shifting the focus away from the objects of moral disapprobation in chapter 1 to the reading/hearing subject who has been up to this point happily identifying with Paul's castigation of someone else. The complex and interesting argument of chapter 1 about certain forms of sin beginning with the 'exchange' of true for false perception and natural for unnatural desire stands, but now has to be applied not to the pagan world alone but to the 'insiders' of the chosen community. Paul is making a primary point not about homosexuality but about the delusions of the supposedly law-abiding.

As I have said, this does nothing to settle the exegetical questions fiercely debated at the moment. But I want to stress that what I am trying to define as a strictly theological reading of Scripture, a reading in which the present community is made contemporary with the world in front of the text, is bound to give priority to the question that the text specifically puts and to ask how the movement, the transition, worked for within the text is to be realised in the contemporary reading community. To move too rapidly to the use of the text to make a general point which does not require the reader to be converted is to step outside what I have been calling the time of the text, the process by which it shapes its question. It is to make the text more passive than active, and so to move away from the stance of the listener, from the stance of the Church as trying to be still enough to hear, and free enough to respond to, God's summons to be his community. Of course, the work of exegesis to establish doctrine and ethics is unavoidable; commentary is always going on. But the first moment of commentary – if this emphasis on the basic character of listening is correct – needs to be the tracing of the 'time' of a text so as to chart where it is moving.

A similar point is made by the Jewish scholar Peter Ochs, whose work on hermeneutics has been so fruitful in recent years. In an essay published in 2005, he sketches the debates within rabbinical tradition around the relationship between the oral and the written Torah – between rabbinical tradition and the text as delivered at Sinai. Rather than treating written Torah as a straightforward, unambiguous declaration of God's will needing minimal interpretation, with oral Torah as an accumulation of commentary that simply lays out what has been handed down by rabbinical transmission from Moses to the present day, we need, Ochs suggests, following the influential Talmudic scholar David Weiss Halivni, and the biblical exegete Michael Fishbane, a model in which oral Torah is indeed continuous with written Torah, not as a kind of supplement but as a continuation of the process already going on in written Torah. The written text is not a synchronic 'surface' of isolated acts of communication; it is a text in which the component parts are in relation with each other, making sense of each other: oral Torah is the ongoing attempt to clarify those relations. 'The Oral

Torah reads the Written Torah, alone, but between its verses.'[3] The divine action that is going on in Scripture is not just a relation between every atomised bit of text and God, but also God elucidating text by text, element by element. Instead of 'the things of the world ... correspond[ing], one for one, to the words of Torah', they correspond to the relations between the words of Torah.[4]

This is a little obscurely worded, but its import is clear. If we speak of the effect of Scripture being the creation of an analogy of situation between the world in front of the text and the world of the current reader/hearer, this is not simply to say that any isolated piece of the text speaks unambiguously and without need of gloss to a current situation. It is rather to claim that the connections between elements of scriptural text, the connections that constitute what I have here been calling its 'movement', will be uncovered in the reader's world as still effecting the same movement and making the same overall demands. The reader who shares the covenant relationship with the first recipients of Torah – to stay with Ochs' argument for the moment – has to draw out the connection between the initial goal of Torah as a whole, which is the establishing of the covenant people in holiness and faithfulness, and the condition of Israel now, so as to find the interpretation 'that speaks most "truly" to the ends of renewing Judaism today, after Destruction'[5] – the destruction of the Temple, the destruction wrought by the Shoah, or any other historical catastrophe that poses a prima facie challenge to the continuity of God's people then and now.

The Christian may seem not to be working with the same kind of issue around radical disruption in continuity – until we reflect on the division of the Testaments itself, with the cross of Jesus as its pivot, as inscribing an analogous problem at the heart of Scripture. Christian Scripture, the New Testament, is already a work of interpretation, a statement of some very paradoxical connections; it is an attempt to chart what is 'between' the texts of Jewish Scripture on which it works. So the form of our twofold canon itself warns against any readings that seek to sidestep the tracing of connections and movement. This is not at all to subscribe to the easy formula that, as Jesus or Paul can apparently overturn the plain meaning of the texts they handle, so the contemporary reader has the liberty to determine what is the most fruitful reading simply on the grounds of what is now purportedly suggested by the Holy Spirit for the health of the present community. This would dissolve the real otherness and integrity of the text. It is not that we are given only a method of interpretation by the form of Scripture – a method that, by pointing us to the conflict and tension between texts, simply leaves us with theologically unresolvable debate as a universal norm for Christian discourse (I make the point partly in order to correct what some have – pardonably – understood as the implication of what I have written elsewhere on this matter). There is a substantive and discernible form. The canon is presented to us as a whole, whose unity is real and coherent, even if not superficially smooth. To quote from Kevin Vanhoozer's recent and magisterial work, 'The canon both recounts the history of God's covenantal dealings with humanity and regulates God's ongoing covenantal relationship with his people ... [I]t is the text that "documents" our covenantal privileges and responsibilities.'[6] We must acknowledge the tensions and internal debates in Scripture; we must also acknowledge the clear sense that the text is presented as a narrative of 'fulfilment' – as one that contains a vision claiming comprehensiveness of meaning. We are to locate ourselves within this set of connections and engagements, the history of Israel, called, exiled, restored, and of Jesus, crucified and risen and alive in the Spirit within the community, and not to regard Scripture as one element in a merely modern landscape of conflicts.

Vanhoozer writes of the Church as 'staging' what Scripture unfolds. Relating this to my earlier discussion, it suggests that the reading community listens so as to be not only summoned into being in the abstract but also called into specific, self-identifying action, action that seeks to embody the Kingdom. And, looking at the full range of scriptural language and demand, this is not just the embodying of formal precept and instruction: it is the reproduction of those patterns of faithful response spelled out in the narrative – further energised and further complicated by the interweaving of patterns of unfaithful and partial response. How are we to re-enact the faith of Abraham or David while recognising that areas of the narrative of Abraham and David are themselves brought under judgement as the text unfolds, judged within the 'movement' of the text? How are we to be faithful to Torah as given to the people of the First Covenant while recognising that the whole notion of Torah is reshaped by the events of Jesus' life and death? Going back for a moment to the text I discussed from the Farewell Discourses a little while ago, we must ultimately say that the reading and hearing required will be found as we find what it is to walk the way of Jesus as he goes to his Father by way of his cross.

A written text inevitably has about it a dual character. It comes before the reader/hearer as a finished product, and so as something that can in some ways be treated as an object. If we are not careful its written character can be misused by working with the text as if it were passive. In contrast to the event of a voice speaking, it can be abstracted from the single occasion when the hearer has no control over what comes to her or him from outside. At the same time, a written text requires re-reading; it is never read for the last time, and it continuously generates new events of interpretation. It is fruitful of renewed communication in a way that the spoken word alone cannot be. So to identify a written text as sacred is to claim that the continuous possibility of re-reading, the impossibility of reading for the last time, is a continuous openness to the intention of God to communicate. Just as the text itself contains re-reading, is almost constituted by re-reading, so that it repeatedly re-creates a movement towards conversion (towards the cross of Jesus, in Christian terms), so the eternal possibility of 'reading again' stands as a warning against ignoring the active 'restlessness' of the text in summoning the reader to change. The writtenness of the text is from one point of view risky as a strategy of communication: it risks the appearance of passivity, and the re-readability of the text risks the appearance of indeterminacy. Yet from another point of view it can be seen as inseparable from the risk of the communication it itself describes as well as enacts – a divine communication that is never without human speech and narrative, never just an interruption of the created continuum, but a pressure upon it that opens up to the divine by the character of its internal relations and connections, the shifting, penitent perspective of a story enacted in time. The writtenness of the text is like the sheer factuality of the historical past as the vehicle of revelation: it is something irreversibly done, but for that very reason continuously inviting or demanding.

A note here on the notion of canonicity so fully discussed by Vanhoozer: were we to treat Scripture's limits as negotiable, we should be challenging the significance of the written character of scriptural revelation. If we were asking whether there could be supplements to Scripture, 'third testaments' and so on, we should be attempting to assess the revelatory claims of various texts that, in the nature of the case, had not been read publicly and communally in the way scriptural texts have been, and therefore not read continuously in anything like the same sense. The closed canon establishes the same texts as the material for public reading for an indefinite time; these texts have the indisputably 'closed' character of the historical past, pointing to an act already definitively enacted, an act to which future reception must respond. Opening the canon (itself a strained use of language if you think about it) would mean that something was being negotiated that was not primarily and essentially a response to an act already performed. We should have a hybrid view of revelation as text plus supplements – additional elements, written or unwritten, uncontrolled by the limits of a text whose identity is fixed as historical. This is the substance of the Reformation objection to certain decadent views of tradition, views decisively rejected by later Catholic thought also.

I have used the language of invitation and summons at a number of points earlier in this essay, and in the final sections of it I want to return to this theme, since it will illuminate some of the issues just touched upon about the specificity and coherence of scriptural revelation.

We noted earlier that the celebration of the Eucharist and the reading of the Bible are the most universal ways in which the Church 'represents' what it is; and both sow the Church as a community committed to listening afresh to its foundational call. The gathering of the assembly for worship is not simply a human routine, however much it may come to look like that. It is, theologically speaking, a moment in which the present activity of God is assumed and responded to.

But to read Scripture in the context of the Eucharist – which has been from the beginning of the Church the primary place for it – is to say that the Word of God that acts in the Bible is a Word directed towards those changes that bring about the Eucharistic community. The summons to the reader/hearer is to involvement in the Body of Christ, the agent of the Kingdom, as we have seen; and that Body is what is constituted and maintained by the breaking of bread and all that this means. For Paul, exploring it in 1 Corinthians, the celebration of the Lord's Supper is strictly bound up with the central character of the community: what is shown in the Eucharist is a community of interdependence and penitent self-awareness, discovering the dangers of partisan self-assertion or uncritical reproduction of the relations of power and status that prevail in the society around. So if Scripture is to be heard as summons or invitation before all else, this is what it is a summons to. And the reading and understanding of the text must be pursued in this light. We ask what change is envisaged or required in the 'time' of any passage of Scripture; and now we can add that whatever change that is in particular, it must make sense in the context of the formation of this kind of community – the Eucharistic Body.

Take Scripture out of this context of the invitation to sit at table with Jesus and be incorporated into his labour and suffering for the Kingdom, and you will be treating Scripture as either simply an inspired supernatural guide for individual conduct or a piece of detached historical record – the typical exaggerations of Biblicist and liberal approaches respectively. For the former, the work of the Spirit is more or less restricted to the transformation of the particular believer; for the latter, the life of the community is where the Spirit is primarily to be heard and discerned, with Scripture an illuminating adjunct at certain points. But grasp Scripture as part of the form taken by the divine act of invitation that summons and establishes the community around the Lord's Table, and the Bible becomes coherent at a new level, as a text whose meaning is most centrally to do with the passage from rivalry and self-assertion, and the enmity with God that is bound up with these, to the community in which each, by the influx of the Spirit, takes responsibility for all, and all for each. The context of the Eucharist, in which everyone present is there simply because they are guests by the free generosity of the host, obliges a reading of Scripture in which what is decisive is always this shared dependence on God's initiative of welcome which removes pride and fear.

But equally, take Scripture out of the Eucharistic context and the Eucharist itself becomes different. Without this anchorage in the history of God's creative welcome as slowly and painfully spelled out in the history of Israel and Jesus, the Eucharist can more readily be distorted into a celebration of what the community now senses itself to be or to have achieved.

It is robbed of the analogy that makes it contempo-
raneous with the founding act – what you might call
the 'Deuteronomic analogy', thinking back to the text
from Deuteronomy 5 discussed earlier ('Not to your
forefathers...'), and so does not see itself as formed
by a divine communication that is in fact conveyed
through human history, through the record of faithful
and unfaithful response. If the Eucharist is properly a
covenant meal, as the founding text declares, it presupposes a connectedness with the history of the covenant
people; it always has (setting aside for a moment the
debates over whether the Last Supper was historically a
Passover meal) a Passover dimension.

Thus Eucharist and Scripture need to be held together
if we are to have an adequate theology of either. The
Eucharist is the primary locus of the listening Church,
the place where it shows itself to be there in response to
the call of God; and the Scripture that embodies that call
has to be read as leading to precisely this point, the existence of a community that embodies Christ and does so
by reflecting his kenotic act. And as I have hinted already,
this must be anchored clearly in a theology of the Spirit,
which holds the two themes together. The Spirit, according to John's Gospel, is the remembrancer, the divine
agency that makes the words of Christ contemporary.
It is the Spirit that incorporates us into one community
with the disciples at the Last Supper and indeed with
the Deuteronomically imagined people of Israel. It is the
Spirit that enables the mutual self-offering that builds up
the Body and that unites the members in the prayer of
the glorified Christ. It is the Spirit that connects the peri-
ods of God's communicative action towards humanity
and thus connects the diverse texts that make up the one

manifold text we call Holy Scripture. The Spirit's work as 'breathing' God's wisdom into the text of Scripture is not a magical process that removes biblical writing from the realm of actual human writing; it is the work of creating one 'movement' out of the diverse historical narratives and textual deposits that represent Israel's and the Church's efforts to find words to communicate God's communication of summons and invitation. The Spirit, through the events of God's initiative, stirs up those words and makes sense of them for the reader/ hearer in the Spirit-sustained community. As Karl Barth insisted,[7] this leaves no ground for breaking up Scripture into the parts we can 'approve' as God-inspired and the parts that are merely human; the whole is human and the whole is offered by God in and through the life of the Body, always shaping and determining the form of that life.

The Spirit in the New Testament, not least in the Johannine tradition, is associated in its fullness with the resurrection of Jesus; and my final point is to note the way in which Eucharist and Scripture alike have to be considered in relation to belief in the resurrection. The Eucharist itself is generally recognised as, among other things, a continuation of Jesus's meal-fellowship with the marginal and disreputable in Israel; by this fellowship, he declares a new way of being Israel that will not restrict membership to those who can satisfy conditions, but rather will be open to all who are ready to be welcomed by him in the name of Israel's God. The Eucharistic encounter is with the Christ who is still today actively defining the people of God simply by his invitation. Seen like this, the Eucharist is not the memorial of past meals with

Jesus but the reality of contemporary response to his hospitality – a hospitality once and for all established as indestructible by the cross and the resurrection, so that what was done in the ministry of Jesus in Galilee and Jerusalem is done constantly in the history of the Church.

But to say that Christ's transforming hospitality is renewed constantly in this history is also to say that Christ continues to speak in and to the community. The community exists because of God's act of communication, as we have seen repeatedly; the resurrection is the persistence of that act. Without belief in the resurrection, our understanding of Scripture is going to be deficient at best. If it is not the present vehicle of God speaking in the risen Christ, it is a record only of God speaking to others. For it to be an address that works directly upon self and community now, it must be given to us as the continuation of the same act, the re-presenting and re-enacting of the same scriptural reality of invitation and the creation of a people defined by justice, mutual service and the liberty to relate to God as Father and faithful partner.

So in sum: what I believe we need for a renewed theological grasp of Scripture is:

(i) the recognition that Scripture is something heard in the event where the community affirms its identity and seeks its renewal;

(ii) the development of the skills needed to explore the analogy and continuity between the world 'in front of' the text and the current context, so as at least to avoid the misuse of texts by abstracting them from the questions they actually put;

(iii) thus also, the discernment of where any given section of Scripture is moving – what are the changes it sets out and proposes for the reader/hearer;

(iv) an understanding that this last is decisively and authoritatively illuminated by the Eucharistic setting of biblical reading;

(v) the consequent holding together of Eucharist and Scripture through a strong doctrine of the Spirit's work in constructing the community of Christ's Body; and

(vi) the recognition that neither Scripture nor Eucharist makes sense without commitment to the resurrection of Jesus as the fundamental condition of a Church whose identity is realised in listening and responding.

Reading Scripture theologically and understanding theologically the process of reading – all this is essentially about seeing Scripture as the vehicle of God's act to bring about conversion. Ultimately, Scripture brings us back to the uniquely creative moment of God's freedom – to the grace of a free self-bestowal that can create what is other and then, by love and welcome, transform that other into a sharer and communicator of the same joyful, generative act. 'The word of life ... [that] we have seen and heard we declare to you, so that you and we together may share in a common life, that life which we share with the Father and his Son Jesus Christ' (1 Jn. 1.1–3).

PART TWO

SHAPING HOLY LIVES

4

God's Workshop

Benedict is, as usual, uncompromisingly prosaic in describing the monastic community as a workshop; it's a place in which we use specific tools – listed with blunt simplicity in chapter 4 of the Rule[1] – which are lent to us by Christ, to be returned on the Last Day, when we receive our wages. It's an image that conjures up a landscape in monochrome, a grey sky, a stone wall: the tools worn smooth with long use and skilfully patched up over time, taken from the shelf each morning until finally hung up when weariness and age arrive. The holy life is one in which we learn to *handle* things, in businesslike and unselfconscious ways, to 'handle' the control of the tongue, the habit of not passing on blame, getting up in the morning and not gossiping. A monastic lifetime is one in which these habits are fitted to our hands. Simone Weil wrote somewhere about how the tool is for the seasoned worker the extension of the hand, not something alien. Benedict's metaphors prompt us to think of a holiness that is like that, an 'extension' of our bodies and our words that we've come not to notice.

In a recent essay on Benedictine Holiness, Professor Henry Mayr-Harting describes it as 'completely undemonstrative, deeply conventual, and lacking any system of expertise.'[2] Very broadly, that is the picture I want to develop with reference to this early and potent image of the workshop and its tools – though I might, while fully understanding the point about expertise, want to think about what sorts of communicable wisdom it also embodies. At this stage, though, perhaps the most important thing to emphasise is the 'deeply conventual': the holiness envisaged by the Rule is entirely inseparable from the common life. The tools of the work are bound up with the proximity of other people – and the *same* other people. As Benedict says at the end of chapter 4, the workshop is itself the very fact of the community's stability. Or, to pick up our earlier language, it is the unavoidable nearness of these others that becomes an extension of ourselves. One of the things we have to grow into unselfconsciousness about is the steady environment of others.

To put it a bit differently, the promise to live in stability is the most drastic way imaginable of recognising the *otherness* of others – just as in marriage. If the other person is there, ultimately, on sufferance or on condition, if there is a time-expiry dimension to our relations with particular others, then we put a limit on the amount of otherness we can manage. Beyond a certain point, we reserve the right to say that our terms must prevail after all. Stability or marital fidelity or any seriously covenanted relationship to person or community resigns that long-stop possibility; which is why it feels so dangerous.

At the very start, then, of thinking about Benedictine holiness, there stands a principle well worth applying to other settings, other relationships – not least the Church itself. How often do we think about the holiness of the

Church as bound up with a habitual acceptance of the otherness of others who have made the same commitment? And what does it feel like to imagine holiness as an unselfconscious getting-used-to-others? The presence of the other as a tool worn smooth and grey in the hand? The prosaic settledness of some marriages, the ease of an old priest celebrating the Eucharist, the musician's relation to a familiar instrument playing a familiar piece – these belong to the same family of experience as the kind of sanctity that Benedict evokes here; undemonstrative, as Mayr-Harting says, because there is nothing to *prove*.

The 'tools of good works' listed include the Golden Rule, several of the Ten Commandments and the corporal works of mercy (clothing the naked, visiting the sick, burying the dead, and so on); but the bulk of them have to do with virtues that can be seen as necessary for the maintenance of stability as a context for growth in holiness. It is as though Benedict were asking, 'What does it take to develop people who can live stably together?' He does not begin by *commending* stability, but by mapping out an environment where the long-term sameness of my company will not breed bitterness, cynicism and fear of openness with one another. If you have to spend a lifetime with the same people, it is easy to create a carapace of habitual response which belongs at the surface level, a set of standard reactions which do not leave you vulnerable. It is the exact opposite of the habitual acceptance of otherness which we were speaking about a little while back, though it can sometimes dangerously resemble it. With a slightly artificial tidiness, we might see the practices Benedict commends for nurturing the stability of the workshop under three imperatives. The monk must be *transparent*; the monk

must be a *peacemaker*; the monk must be *accountable*.
Let's look at these in turn.

Transparency: those who belong to a community such
as Benedict describes are required to 'rid your heart of
all deceit' (4.24 in the list of 'tools'), and, intriguingly,
'never give a hollow greeting of peace' – not to give,
literally, 'false peace' (4.25); to acknowledge their own
culpability in any situation of wrong (4.42–3 – a principle regularly stressed by the Desert Fathers); to be daily
mindful of death (4.47); to deal without delay with evil
thoughts, breaking them against the rock of Christ, and
to make them known to the spiritual father (4.50–1 –
again a familiar precept in the desert). These and other
precepts suggest that one of the basic requirements of
the life is honesty. First, honesty about yourself: it is
necessary to know how to spot the chains of fantasy
(which is exactly what 'thoughts', *logismoi*, meant for
the Desert Fathers), to understand how deeply they are
rooted in a weak and flawed will, and to make your
soul inhospitable to untruth about yourself. Exposure
of your fantasies to an experienced elder is an indispensable part of learning the skills of diagnosis here. In the
background are the analyses of Evagrius and Cassian,
pinpointing what simple boredom can do in a life where
ordinary variety of scene and company is missing. The
mind becomes obsessional, self-enclosed, incapable of
telling sense from nonsense; the reality of the other in
its unyielding difference is avoided by retreat into the
private world where your own preference rules unre-
stricted. Hence the stress on making thoughts known: it
is a simple way of propping open the door of the psyche,
a way of making incarnate the consciousness that God
sees us with complete clarity in every situation (4.49).

To become in this way open to your own scrutiny, through the listening ministry of the trusted brother or sister, is to take the first step towards an awareness of the brother or sister that is not illusory or comforting. The recommendation against 'false peace', I suspect, belongs in this context: one of the ways in which we can retreat into privacy is the refusal to admit genuine conflict, to seek for a resolution that leaves us feeling secure without ever engaging the roots of difference. If we are to become transparent, we must first confront the uncomfortable fact that we are not naturally and instantly at peace with all.

This *could* of course read like a commendation of the attitude which declines reconciliation until justice (to me) has been fully done; but I don't think this is what Benedict is thinking of. The recommendation follows two precepts about anger and resentment (4.22,23), which, taken together with the warning against false peace, suggests that being wary of facile reconciliation is not about a suspicion of whether the other has adequately made reparation, but about whether I have fully acknowledged and dealt with my own resentment. It is a hesitation over my honesty about peace, not the other's acceptability.

One of the most profound books I know on the subject of Christian community is the late Donald Nicholl's wonderful journal of his time as Rector of the Ecumenical Institute at Tantur, between Jerusalem and Bethlehem.[3] In it he records a conversation with a visiting Spanish scholar, who observes that many members of the community have come 'with much heavy matter of unforgiveness and resentment lodged inside them from previous experience ... it is precisely those who talk most about community-building who block the flow, because they are the ones least aware of the matter of unforgiveness that they are carrying around with them, like a lead ball attached to their waists'.[4] Is this what is meant by 'false peace' – to talk about community-building as an alibi for addressing the inner weight of anger and grief? And it isn't irrelevant that Nicholl contrasts the attitude of the Catalan Benedictines who live at the core of the community with that of the more transient scholars, who all come with an agenda that connects to other settings and other communities; the issues are different for those who are not living with stability.

All this gives something of a new edge to the commendation that the monk should be a peacemaker. The precepts are clear enough: there should be no retaliation (4.29–32), no malicious gossip (4.40), no hatred or envy or party spirit (4.65–8). And the climactic items in the list of tools make the priority of peacemaking very plain indeed:

72. Pray for your enemies out of love for Christ.
73. If you have a dispute with someone, make
    peace with him before the sun goes down.
74. And finally, never lose hope in God's mercy.

Stability requires this daily discipline of mending; it is the opposite of an atmosphere in which one's place always has to be fought for, where influence and hierarchy are a matter of unceasing struggle. As Professor Mayr-Harting notes, the idea that position in the community depends on seniority of entry (ch. 63) may seem banal to us now, but it was a most unusual way of understanding hierarchy in late antiquity. It seems obvious because the Rule has had such a sustained impact on the institutions of our culture. But we need to note that the same chapter which establishes the principle of seniority also insists that specific responsibilities in the community do *not* depend on age but on the discernment of the abbot, and that the order of age should not become a ground for insisting on rights and rank. It is a delicate balance, but one whose goal is evidently to secure an ethos in which open conflict over position or influence is less likely. And while rumour suggests that monastic communities are not completely immune to power struggles, the point is that the Rule provides a structure which will always challenge any assumption that conflict is the 'default position' in common life.

To put this another way, what the Rule outlines is what is to be the 'currency' of the community. All communities need a medium of exchange, a language that assures their members that they are engaged in the same enterprise. It involves common stories and practices, things that you can expect your neighbour to understand without explanation, ways and styles of doing and saying things. Once again, Donald Nicholl has a pertinent story; this time, he is listening to a visiting English priest, who relates the experience of a university mission. Fr Aidan is, naturally, interested in what the 'currency' of the university is, and he spends time trying to pick up what people talk about and how. '"And eventually", Aidan said, "one day the penny dropped. What did those people exchange with one another when they met? You'd be surprised – they exchanged grievances. So the currency of that University is grievance."'

Nicholl comments by translating this into the image of the circulation of the blood in a body: what you receive is what you give, what you put into the circulation.

'If you put in grievance, you will get back grievance.'[5] And he refers to an elderly religious in Yorkshire, unobtrusive and to the untutored eye rather idle; but it is he 'who sets the currency of goodness and kindness circulating through that community'.[6] Without some such input into the 'circulation', communities will be at best dry and at worst deadly.

Peacemaking, then, is more than a commitment to reconciling those at odds. On its own, a passion for reconciliation, we have seen, can be a displacement for unresolved angers and resentments. What it may put into circulation is anxiety or censoriousness, certainly a situation of tense untruth when there is pressure to 'make peace' at all costs. The peace which the Rule envisages is more like this 'currency' we've been thinking about, a habit of stable determination to put into the life of the body something other than grudges. And for that to happen, the individual must be growing in the transparency we began with, aware of the temptations of drama, the staging of emotional turbulence in which the unexamined ego is allowed to rampage unchecked.

It's all quite difficult for us in the twenty-first century. We have been told – rightly – that it is bad to deny and repress emotion; equally rightly, that it is poisonous for us to be passive under injustice. The problem, which half an hour on the street outside will confirm, and five minutes watching 'reality' programmes on television will reinforce as strongly as you could want, is that we so readily take this reasonable corrective to an atmosphere of unreality and oppression as an excuse for promoting the dramas of the will. The denial of emotion is a terrible thing; what takes time is learning that the positive path is the education of emotion, not its uncritical indulgence, which actually locks us far more firmly in our mutual isolation. Likewise, the denial of rights is a terrible thing; and what takes time to learn is that the opposite of oppression is not a wilderness of litigation and reparation but the nurture of concrete, shared respect. If concern with right and reparation fills our horizon, the Rule suggests, the one thing we shall not attain is unselfconsciousness – respect as another of those worn-smooth tools that are simply an extension of the body.

None of this is learned without the stability of the workshop. The community that freely promises to live together before God is one in which both truthfulness and respect are enshrined. *I promise that I will not hide from you – and that I will also at times help you not to hide from me or from yourself. I promise that your growth towards the good God wants for you will be a wholly natural and obvious priority for me; and I trust that you have made the same promise.* We have a lifetime for this. Without the promise, the temptation is always for the ego's agenda to surface again, out of fear that I shall be abandoned if the truth is known, fear that I have no time or resource to change as it seems I must. No-one is going to run away; and the resources of the community are there on my behalf.

I realise that I am describing the Body of Christ, not just a Benedictine community. But how often do we understand the promises of baptism as bringing us into this sort of group? How often do we think of the Church as a natural place for honesty, where we need not be afraid? Hence the need for these localised, even specialised workshops, which take their place between two dangerous and illusory models of human life together. On the one hand is what some think the Church is (including, historically, quite a lot of those who actually run it...): an institution where control is a major priority, where experts do things that others can't, where orderly common life depends on a faintly magical command structure. On the other hand is the modern and postmodern vision of human sociality: a jostle of plural commitments and hopes, with somewhat arbitrary tribunals limiting the damage of conflict and securing the rights of all to be themselves up to the point where they trespass on the territory of others – so that the other is virtually bound to be seen as the source of frustration. The community of the Rule assumes that the point of authority is not to mediate between fixed clusters of individual interest but to attend to the needs and strengths of each in such a way as to lead them forward harmoniously (as the chapters on the abbot's ministry make plain); and it also assumes that each member of the community regards relation with the others as the material of their own sanctification, so that it is impossible to see the other as necessarily a menace. Neither simply hierarchical (in the sense of taking for granted an authority whose task is to secure uniformity in accord with a dominant will) nor individualistic, the Rule reminds the Church of how counter-cultural its style of common life might be.

But we have already begun to move into thinking about my third element in Benedictine holiness, *accountability*. At the simplest level, this is almost identical with the transparency already discussed; but it is made very clear that the exercise of the abbot's rule has to be characterised by accountability. Although what the abbot says must be done, without complaint (ch. 5), the abbot is adjured at some length to recall his answerability before God, his call to be the image of Christ in the monastery and to 'leaven' the minds of those under his care, and his duty to ignore apparent claims of status among the monks. His work is seen as, centrally, one of instruction and formation, and Mayr-Harting is absolutely right to see this as grounded in the language of St Paul: authority exists so as to create adult persons in Christ's likeness, and all discipline is directed to this end – with the added emphasis in the Rule of attention to the requirements of different temperaments (ch. 27 is the most humanly subtle of the various accounts of this in the text).

The abbot makes distinctions not on the basis of visible difference (rich or poor, slave or free) but on the basis of his discernment of persons. You could say that his accountability is both to God and to the spiritual realities of the people he deals with. And this perhaps fills out the significance of the idea of accountability in the Rule as a whole: we are answerable to the concreteness of the other. Obedience to the abbot is the most obvious form of this, but that obedience itself refers to the life and health of the whole community, since the abbot exercises discipline only in that context, and is ultimately accountable in those terms. In short, everyone in the community that the Rule envisages is responsible both to and for everyone else – in different modes, depending on the different specific responsibilities they hold, but nonetheless sharing a single basic calling in this respect. The workshop is manifestly a collaborative venture with the aim of 'mending vices and preserving love' (Prologue).

So the Rule envisages holiness as a set of habits – like goodness in general, of course, but not reducible to goodness only. The holy person is not simply the one

who keeps the commandments with which the catalogue
of tools for good works begins, but one who struggles to
live without deceit, their inner life manifest to guides and
spiritual parents, who makes peace by addressing the
roots of conflict in him or herself, and, under the direction of a skilled superior, attempts to contribute their
distinctive gifts in such a way as to sustain a healthy
'circulation' in the community. You can see why Benedict
is clear about the need for long probation of the intend-
ing solitary, and why he is so hard on wanderers, who
can never have adequate experience of living with the
same people, becoming habituated to charity with these
particular, inescapable neighbours (ch. 1). Until stability has soaked in, it isn't much use reading the Desert
Fathers or Cassian or Basil: to borrow a notion from
Jacob Needleman's remarkable *Lost Christianity*,[7] the
words of the Fathers are addressed to 'people who don't
yet exist'. To know even a little of what the great spiritual teachers are saying, you need to have lived through
the education of instinct that the Rule outlines. It is just
worth noting that there are 72 'tools of good works'
to correspond to the first 72 chapters of the Rule; it
is the 73rd chapter that points forward to the greater
challenges of the Fathers. And this suggests that the 72
tools are precisely, like the 72 chapters, a preparation
for hearing what the Fathers have to say, a method by
which persons who can hear the questions may come
into existence.

The product of the workshop is people who are really
there; perhaps it's as simple as that. What Benedict is
interested in producing is people who have the skills to
diagnose all inside them that prompts them to escape
from themselves in the here and now. Just as much as

in the literature of the desert – despite his insistence that he is working on a different and lower level – Benedict regards monastic life as a discipline for being where you are, rather than taking refuge in the infinite smallness of your own fantasies. Hence he can speak, in one of those images that continue to resonate across the centuries, of the expansion of the heart that obedience to the Rule will bring. The life is about realising great matters in small space: *Cael neuadd fawr / Rhwng cyfyng furiau* – 'inhabiting a great hall between narrow walls'. That is the definition of life itself offered by the Welsh poet Waldo Williams in one of his best-known poems, and it is not a bad gloss on the Rule.

But I have already hinted at some of what makes the Rule hard reading these days, and in the last bit of these reflections I want to draw out just a little more on this, so as to suggest where the Rule is salutary reading for us, individually and corporately. The idea fundamental to the Rule (and to practically all serious religious writing) that there are some good things which are utterly inaccessible without the taking of time is probably the greatest brick wall. And it is not just a matter of personal neurosis; given the 24-hour pattern of news provision, we are discouraged very strongly from any suspicion that the significance of events might need time to understand. After the Iraq war, those who were doubtful of its wisdom or legitimacy were urged to retract, since it had, after all, been won; it didn't seem to be easy to convey that until it could be seen how relations of various kinds were properly mended it might be premature to speak of victory – even of endings. It is rather symptomatic of our urgency in wanting what we these days call closure. But the truth is that serious and deep meanings only emerge as we look and listen, as we accompany a long story in its unfolding – whether we are thinking about the meaning of a life (mine or anyone's) or the meaning of a period in international affairs. Stability is still the key, a *staying with* that gives us the opportunity ourselves to change as we accompany, and so to understand more fully.

And what we have been thinking about in relation to peacemaking has an uncomfortable pertinence just at the moment. Are we capable, as Western societies, of peace that is not 'false' in Benedict's terms? That is, are we sufficiently alert to the agenda we are bringing to international conflict – resentments, the sense of half-buried impotence that sits alongside the urge to demonstrate the power we do have, the desire to put off examining the unfinished business in our own societies? And, for that matter, there is the falsity that can also afflict would-be peacemakers, who are more concerned with condemning what's wrong than with planning for what might change things, and who derive some comfort from knowing where evil lies (i.e. in someone else, some warmongering monster). What do we do to help our culture discover or recover habits of honesty? Is there a healing of the 'circulation'? 'Peace work', writes Donald Nicholl,[8] 'demands a far higher degree of self-discipline, spiritual preparation and self-knowledge than we are generally prepared to face.'

And as for accountability – we tend these days to pride ourselves on taking this seriously; we have intro-duced the notion of audit into most of what we do, and are encouraged to challenge anything that looks like non-accountable exercising of authority. But I suspect that all this is actually rather a long way from what the Rule has in mind. First of all, the accountability of the Rule depends on a clear common understanding of what everyone is answerable to: the judgement of Christ. The Rule has nothing resembling a speculative Christology; but all the lines lead to Christ, the central instance of authority rightly used and attention rightly directed to God and the immediate other. There is no interest at all in the Rule in challenging authority on abstract principle. What there is is a clear commitment to listening, as a central and necessary aspect of making decisions, listening even to the most junior (ch. 3); the possibility of explaining difficulties and asking for consideration of special circumstances (ch. 68); and the repeated insistence that the abbot is measured by and must measure himself by the standard of Christ's pastoral service, with its focal principle of self-gift for the sake of the life of the other. When abbatial decisions are made, the monk must ultimately obey; but the context remains one in which we are being urged to think not about an audit, in the sense of an assessment of whether the processes in use are delivering the desired results, but about the degree to which the community is genuinely working with a shared focus and common language, in which both discussion and decision are possible.

The Rule is in no way a primitive democratic document, and its appeals to obedience are undoubtedly counter-cultural these days. But what the discomfort arising from this misses is the sense of standing together before Christ, becoming used to Christ's scrutiny *together*. In this way, we both see ourselves under Christ's judgement and see others under Christ's mercy; and we are urged not to despair of that mercy even for ourselves. Not to despair of mercy is the last of the tools of good works; we could say that the final point of accountability before Christ was that we should have as the extension of our natural bodily being the habit of hope, trust in the possibilities of compassion. And the abbot is in a unique position to put that into circulation.

What the 'audit' culture lacks is usually a positive shared focus. We have a clear sense of what counts as breach of responsibility, and usually a clear (if often artificially clear) account of what effective exercise of responsibility should produce. What we don't often have is the tacit or explicit reference to the shared focus of meaning that allows real mutuality in the life of the group under authority. Challenges belong in the context – yet again – of a stability that guarantees we all know what we are talking about and what we hope for.

So the Rule's sketch of holiness and sanity puts a few questions to us, as Church and culture. It suggests that one of our main problems is that we don't know where to find the stable relations which would allow us room to grow without fear. The Church which ought to embody not only covenant with God but covenant with each other does not always give the feeling of a community where people have unlimited time to grow with each other, nourishing and challenging. We have little incentive to be open with each other if we live in an ecclesial environment where political conflict and various kinds of grievance are the dominant currency. And, believers and unbelievers, we'd like to be peacemakers without the inner work which alone makes peace something more than a pause in battle. We are bad at finding that elusive balance between corrupt and collusive passivity which keeps oppression alive and the litigious obsessiveness that continually asks whether I am being attended to as I deserve. And no, I don't have a formula for resolving that; I only ask that we find ways of reminding ourselves that there is a problem.

So we'd better have some communities around that embody the stability that is at the heart of all this. 'Each [religious] house is meant to be a model – an "epiphany" rather – of the condition of mankind reconciled in Christ', wrote Fergus Kerr in an essay around 1970.[9] And he goes on to say that this is impossible unless we face the real condition of unreconciledness in and between us; which is why religious houses are not always exactly easy places ... But in the terms of these reflections we should have to say that without the stability the work isn't done; the tools don't become extensions of the hand in such a way that the other's reality really and truly ceases to be an intrusion and a threat. How right Benedict was to say that it is only when community life has done its work that someone should be allowed to take up the solitary life: only when the other is not a problem can solitude be Christlike – otherwise it is an escape, another drama.

A monochrome picture? Perhaps, but the self-indulgent technicolour of what are sometimes our preferred styles needs some chastening. The workshop is at the end of the day a solid and tough metaphor for that spirituality which is a lifetime's labour, yet also an expansion of the heart; just as all good physical work is an expansion of the body into its environment, changing even as it brings about change. Holiness is a much-patched cloth, a smooth-worn tool at least as much as it is a blaze of new light; because it must be finally a state we can live with and in, the hand fitted to the wood forgetful of the join.

5

Urban Spirituality

It's said fairly often that the biblical narrative begins in a garden and ends in a city. Something about the way God leads us through history is linked, it seems, with our growth towards a situation in which we take a more and more creative role in shaping our environment – not just in cultivating the natural environment in which God has placed us, like Adam, but in building a complex kind of home that is shared by others, with whom we have to negotiate, whose concerns we have to ponder and interact with. The garden is a good image for some aspects of our growth with God. It may seem the most obvious image (*The Garden of the Soul* was, after all, the title of the most influential English book of Catholic piety in the modern era). But it is the *City* of God that dominates the most sophisticated reflection on the nature of God's community.

And here we are likely to feel a bit of dissonance. Cities these days are not the soberly elegant city states of mediaeval Italy, or even the burgeoning, buzzing (and hideously polluted) industrial and commercial centres of the nineteenth century. 'Urbanisation' is now one of the words that most vividly describes the demographic crisis and human tragedy of late modernity. It goes with globalisation: it signifies the inexorable drift towards structures and landscapes – including landscapes of economic relations and social possibilities – that are in various ways inhuman. These are structures and land-scapes that proclaim the powerlessness of individuals and of small-scale societies to exercise any creative role in moulding the environment. They speak of spaces that are not mapped or shaped with human beings in mind – uncharted and undifferentiated space, where no-one feels at home. How can the contemporary city be a place where the spirit can flourish?

But it is hard to imagine the process going backwards. At the very least, we can't now imagine a situation where communities stop being mobile and mixed. We have become used to cities as places of variety – places where those with purchasing power can exercise the maximal amount of consumer freedom; but also places where difference between groups need not always break down into savage hostility, because there is room for some space between communities. It is true that this collapses pretty often, and that new tribal loyalties are created and so new conflicts; but there is something about the space of urban existence that makes it attractive (and always has made it attractive) for the minority. Your life is less likely to be seen as a threat by a close-knit and quite homogeneous community. And precisely because minorities find a voice in urban life, they can begin to influence majorities: radical change comes from urban life rather than rural.

Urban life, then, is at once dangerous and creative; at once destructive of much that is humanly significant and a seedbed in which change can germinate and people become able to think of new possibilities. If we are trying to be clear about how to pray and how to be a disciple in the modern city, we have to avoid equally a sentimental view of urban life in terms of entrepreneurial energy and fresh chances, and an apocalyptic picture of unrelieved inhumanity. We have to ask what the real choices are and how they serve the uncovering of God's image.

So what follows is at best a sketch of the sort of themes and concerns that might inform an 'urban spirituality' today. It is not a programme or a prescription: one of the lessons that has to be learned is that it won't do to impose an agenda from outside. Urban populations need to understand for themselves where and who they are and what their possibilities might be. And the role of the Church needs some careful thinking through. Sam Wells, in a particularly insightful essay on the role of the Church in community regeneration,[1] has noted the problem that can arise if the Church is seen as one interest group among others, bidding competitively for scarce resources, or seeking to control the self-definition of communities. The contribution of the Church must always be something on another level from that of the various bodies struggling for dominance and access; it must simply offer a radically different imaginative landscape, in which people can discover possibilities of change – and perhaps of 'conversion' in the most important sense, a 'turning around' of values and priorities that grows from trust in God.

Wells suggests ways in which the distinctive practices of the Church – baptism, communion, Bible reading and prayer – both signal and make possible alternative accounts of what life might be. Building on what he says, I want to suggest a few possible priorities for those concerned with the life of the spirit in the modern city.

The first has to do with the use and organisation of *time*. As we have noted, one of the characteristics of the modern urban environment is the growing homogenisation of *space*: people live in settings that are more 'flattened' and undifferentiated than the village and the small town. Mass housing, the modern insistence on 'zoning' in urban planning (so that residential and retail properties aren't found side by side), and the general gulf between the processes of planning and the decisions of actual inhabitants, mean that a lot of (especially newer) urban landscapes are interchangeable. The prevailing patterns of retail commerce reinforce this: the same retail chains are found everywhere, with identical merchandise. So one of the first questions about the spirit and the city must be what can be restored to a differentiated style; what in the environment can speak of difference, of individualities that are not just exchangeable the world over, and so of real exchange between diverse persons and communities.

For the Christian, this matters because of our belief that the optimal form of Christian community, the Body of Christ, is one in which diversity of gifts and the movement of giving and receiving are all-important. If people are to be brought a little closer to this optimal community style, there must be ways of affirming and celebrating difference. Religious communities are all agreed that time needs breaking up, punctuating, by festival (and fasting too) – by rhythms that shape the passage of time and recognise different emotions, different stages in growth; that recognise that dimension of human living which involves process and the shifts of 'climate' in the life of mind and heart. Breaking up time into weeks and months and years is only the tip of the

iceberg; all societies until the modern age have structured the weeks and the years in more elaborate ways,
usually coinciding with the agricultural year. A society
that has moved away from these rhythms either becomes
obsessed with using time 'profitably' – or it sets out
to rediscover rhythms of celebration that can survive
the urban environment, the relative distance from the
change of the seasons that is inevitable in city life.

Andrew Shanks's splendid and provocative book,
God and Modernity,[2] puts a case for 'calendar reform' –
for a new civic consciousness that organises time around
freshly thought-out historical commemorations (the
fall of the Berlin Wall, the legacy of the slave trade and
its ending). This, he suggests, would give us a corporate sense both of a present time that had pauses and
movements, like a musical composition, and a past time
that had both triumphs and failures. But this in turn
suggests – whatever may become of such proposals at
the level of a whole nation – that an urban environment
needs the same rhythm of movement and pause at the
local level. One of the things that anyone concerned with
this should reflect on is what can be done to make public
and celebrate reflectively the things that a community
regards as defining and important. Perhaps it's often a
matter of hanging some of this on to existing festival
dates in the Church's calendar – commemorating specific
local trauma in Holy Week, using Mothering Sunday to
say something about the joys and challenges of parent-
ing in a community, perhaps to remember the local
difficulties or tragedies of children, certainly to make
a point about communication between generations. It
is certainly not about replacing the Church's calendar
with something completely other. It is both seeking new

and independent commemorations and, where appropriate, including local and particular history within the Church's story – while being careful not to swallow it, exploit it or make it no more than an illustration of some pre-existing Christian moral. A hard task, but not impossible. And the ethnic and religious variety of the modern urban scene means that the available religious calendars are not going to be exclusively Christian; nothing to regret there, as many pastors and workers in the urban context would testify.

The weekend may be a lost cause in many communities, thanks to that triumph of functional and acquisitive philosophy that was the legitimising of Sunday trading. But this does not mean that we can or should give up on the question of how to structure the time in which people live, and the weekly rhythm is not the only one possible, however much we might feel nostalgic for it. Urban society's time needs punctuations, if it is not to become a view without landmarks. There are matters to celebrate and mourn together, if we can listen and find out; and as we do it may become possible to find a way of marking times and seasons that is not artificial.

A second possibility. The urban landscape is characteristically characterless. What, then, gives 'character'? I have a recollection of a woman in a South Welsh urban setting who had decided (she lived alone and could determine her domestic timetable) to set aside her small living room as a place where other women in the neighbourhood could come for silence at almost any time in the week. If they turned up, they could sit alone or they could be quietly accompanied. In a landscape without *spatial* 'pauses', gaps for reflection, holy places, she had simply decided to create something of this sort, in a prosaic and accessible way. So the question is, Who in a community might have the resource (physical and spiritual) to provide space of this kind? There are often those who are recognisable as having made space in themselves, who, in a pressurised and crowded human environment, bring a sense of giving others room to breathe. How can they be helped and supported to keep open the offer their lives imply? And can their gifts be linked with actual places, like my friend's living room? This is a different question from one that is often raised in this context, the question (equally important) of how you learn to recognise the places that as a matter of fact are regarded as significant public space in a community, even as holy, charged with meaning or memory. But it is a question worth addressing. And somewhere between the provision of space for quiet in households and the recognition of publicly accessible significant space is a phenomenon that seems to have become more prominent in recent years – an interest mostly among voluntary groups in reclaiming small public spaces as memorial gardens, protected places for quiet. The vastly impressive summer campaign, 'Soul in the City', in which young people of Christian conviction descend in great numbers on an urban environment in need of help and reclamation, quite often involves projects of this sort. And their work is a regular reminder of the more general point that the message that an environment is in some sense simply *manageable*, that it does not have to spiral out of control as far as basic cleanliness and useability are concerned, is a serious element of what the good news can entail in a physically degraded setting.

A third area is perhaps more obvious. Urban life is lived under the sign of anonymous exchange; should not any community concerned with spiritual health therefore be on the watch for those forms of exchange that avoid the anonymous? This is not to suggest that the Church become an enthusiastic sponsor of the black market that is the main form of economic activity in a good many areas of acute urban deprivation! Black markets are really just another kind of unaccountable and exploitative power mechanism. But local trading schemes, micro-credit initiatives and so on are structures with well-defined and close local accountability, a good record in developing skills and restoring a sense of limited but real control over economic circumstances, and a low level of capital and organisational outlay. They generate self-respect and broad and forward-looking vision for oneself and others. They are something that a local faith community can contribute to very effectively, offering a ready-made pool of volunteers. More importantly, though, they represent a challenge to the assumption of urban modernity that serious power and effective organisation always has to be centralised. And, as I have suggested, there are good theological reasons for resisting this assumption, to the degree that it takes for granted a pattern of social relation that has little room for mutuality.

I mention in passing here the 'Habitat for Humanity' schemes of house-building that have been so successful in many American urban settings, but have still to be taken fully seriously in the UK. Here, as with local micro-credit, the point is to give a degree of choice and control to local groups that is *not* simply a form of generalised consumer choice. In a context where a majority in the community have limited economic freedom, what is needed is not a range of options offered by a mass provider, but a few realistic paths for action that will affirm that it is possible after all to have a creative impact on your environment.

All I have said so far is based on the assumption that the search for spiritual seriousness in the modern and postmodern urban setting takes place against a material background designed with minimal attention to the needs of human community. The strategies outlined inevitably have an air of damage limitation. And in any comprehensive look at the spirit in the city, we need also to think about a possible future in which it would not always be necessary to take for granted that the physical environment would be inimical to ordinary human flourishing. The challenge is how to get theology on to the agenda of planning, locally and nationally (though without necessarily letting on that it *is* theology).

We live in an age of paradox. We have as a culture become very interested in 'sick buildings', in the mistakes made in the recent past about where and how natural light is allowed in, in feng shui and all that goes with it, in the inadequacy of Le Corbusier's infamous definition of a house as 'a machine for living in'; yet we persist in habits of large-scale planning (and indeed in the construction of public buildings) that suggest we are really gnostics who believe in a total separation of body and spirit. But we ought to have learned that the spirit's welfare is not a subject we can sensibly discuss without both a science and a wisdom of the environment. We have to take seriously what physical and psychological research tells us about the effects of certain material structures on how we think and feel about ourselves; and we need to have a positive vision of humanity and of what a freely co-operative humanity might require – a vision shaped not just by guesswork and vague good-will, but by that fundamental Christian conviction about the Body of Christ as the best form of human togetherness.

6

Forbidden Fruit: Sexuality and Spirituality in Perspective

Perhaps the first thing to say is that there *isn't* really very much in the way of what we should think of as sexual ethics in the New Testament. There are meditations and recommendations to do with marriage, and there are some stark observations about celibacy; there are a few scattered remarks about vaguely defined 'impurity' or 'uncleanness' of behaviour, *porneia*, which seems to refer to anything from adultery to prostitution; there are, in the writings ascribed to St Paul, three disparaging references to sexual activity between men. Jesus is recorded as following a strict line on the admissibility of a man deciding to dissolve his marriage (not exactly a discussion of divorce in the modern sense), and refers in passing to *porneia* as one of the evils that come from the inner core of the self. And that's about it. The overall impression is certainly that sexual activity is an area of moral risk, and that nothing outside marriage is to be commended. But it is, when you look at the texts, surprisingly difficult to find this spelled out in any detail, explored or defended.

Or is it so surprising? We easily forget that the Christian Scriptures were not written to answer *our* questions.

We assume that there is an area of human experience called 'sexuality', which is of immense importance, something which needs to be sorted out before anyone can claim to be leading a mature and fulfilled human life. But the world of Jesus and Paul would not have recognized such language. They knew about marriages as complicated bundles of economic and family arrangements, ideally but not always involving mutual affection and stability; they knew that young males were most unlikely to resist promptings towards sexual involvement, and generally did their best to stop this damaging excessively the tidiness of arrangements about marriage; they assumed that women were unreliable and easily swayed by emotion, so needed protection from casual liaisons, in order to be eligible for a 'good' marriage; they knew about the situation in which an older man took up a younger one, offering him patronage and instruction in return for a modicum of bodily pleasure. They would have been puzzled to see all this brought together under a single heading, or to be asked about their 'sexuality'. There was desire, there were acts of sexual intimacy, there was the important public bond of marriage, indispensable in sorting out issues about property rights and inheritance. These things did not need to have much to do with each other.

In a rather odd way, Christianity itself bears some of the responsibility for the emergence of a unified approach to sexual experience and activity – chiefly by giving enormous and increasing importance to sexual abstinence. Early Christians proudly proclaimed their distinctiveness by pointing to the fact that at least a substantial proportion of their number renounced all sexual activity; this was regarded – along with the courage of Christians in the face of death – as one of the proofs of the supernatural power of faith. And inevitably the variety of things renounced – marriage, but also youthful affairs, casual sex with slaves, male or female, and the use of prostitutes – tended to be lumped together as, after all, a single area of human behaviour, and one that was inherently deeply compromising for a person living by faith in Christ and in hope of life everlasting. Despite what a number of silly textbooks and journalistic surveys tell you, the majority of early Christian writers didn't think sex *as such* was evil; they simply thought it was too complex for comfort; it weighed you down, tangled your thoughts and emotions unhelpfully, and – well, at the end of the day, wasn't it just a bit ... undignified? Few of the early Christians sound like neurotics obsessed with the filth of sex (some do); most are simply rather snobbish about it. It's vulgar and messy; best not to bother.

But this is already some way from what the New Testament actually says. For Jesus and Paul, the problem isn't that sex is irrational or vulgar, but that certain kinds of bonding will turn out to be too all-consuming for at least *some* of the citizens of God's Kingdom. Jesus seems to commend celibacy for 'those who can manage it', particularly those who are called to the life of wandering preachers – the Twelve and their immediate successors. Even there, the rule is obviously not absolute: St Paul mentions in passing that St Peter was accompanied on his travels by his wife. Paul assumes the end of the world is due very shortly: the serious Christian may well feel that being encumbered with a family to provide for might get in the way of what needs doing in the short time left. And Paul evidently doesn't think any other form of sexual union is worth discussing in this context.

What is baffling and sometimes outrageous to the modern reader is just this assumption that, in certain circumstances, sex can't matter all *that* much. And I want to suggest that the most important contribution the New Testament can make to our present understanding of sexuality may be precisely in this unwelcome and rather chilling message. We come to the New Testament eagerly looking for answers, and we meet a blank or quizzical face: why is *that* the all-important problem? Not all human goods are possible all the time, and it would be a disaster to think that there was some experience without which *nothing* else made sense. Only if sexual intimacy is seen as the last hiding-place of real transcendence, to borrow a phrase from the American novelist, Walker Percy, could we assume that it mattered above all else. But we are now in a cultural situation where there really isn't much left of transcendence for a lot of people, and they have to take what they can get. To quote Walker Percy once again, it may be that for more and more people sex is practically the only way they can feel sure they are really *there*, really the object of another's attention. Other cultures didn't and don't share that anxiety: it's really quite important to be reminded of that from time to time, to ask whether having the reassurances of sexual intimacy would be the first priority in times of profound crisis or corporate suffering, whether we'd give it higher priority in extreme moments than attention to pain or to beauty.

All right; but that doesn't help much with the average situation for most of us, where we're not in crisis, not expecting the end of the world and not conscious of a vocation to be a wandering preacher. And what we've just said in fact still presupposes that sex is a very heavily charged, significant matter, if it can in some ways compete, as we know it does, with the claims of other deeply serious areas of our humanity. So let's take as read the way in which the New Testament comes to us at an angle from our expectations, and pursue what it specifically says about what we'd call the sexual in our experience. Paul is, as always, fearfully unsystematic, but he hints here and there at a rationale for his somewhat throwaway remarks on marriage and other matters. His major contribution is 1 Corinthians 7: if this had been lost in the post, Christian ethics would have been very different, since there is more here on sexual relationships than in all the rest of the New Testament. Yes, celibacy is a good idea if you can manage it; but abstinence is hard work, and not a very good idea *within* marriage. In marriage, says Paul rather startlingly, neither party any longer owns their own body; it is given to another. This is ambiguous in its implications, as several recent commentators have said: 'ownership' still leaves us with a problem about sex as the exercise of power, even if it is shared out. But it overturns one very fundamental assumption of Paul's Jewish and Greek environment – that the woman has no power and no independent desire in the married relation. Paul allows her initiative and responsibility, not only duties; but the central image is one in which partners *renounce* the idea that they have rights to be exercised at each other's expense, and are able to entrust themselves to the care of another. My *right* is to be honoured, not coerced, by my partner, but I can only express this by allowing that my own 'power' in this relationship is given purely for the purpose of returning the same honour. Neither is free *from* the other; each is free *for* the other.

The Letter to the Ephesians, which may or may not be directly from Paul's hand, makes the connection with the way God in Jesus Christ deals with us: by self-gift and self-sacrifice – though the writer goes on to make a less clear connection between the wife's response of obedience and the Church's obedience to Christ. If we were developing the analogy in terms of what is said in 1 Corinthians, we might expect some sense that the marriage relation could image Christ's self-gift on *both* sides. But another insight into a possible method for looking at sexual intimacy can be teased out: Christians are meant to reflect the form and style of divine action in all they do; sexual activity is no exception. If God acts for us by letting go of a divine power that is abstract and unilateral and comes in Jesus's life to set us free for working with Jesus and praying with Jesus, this suggests strongly that a sexual partnership that is unequal, that represents power exercised by one person trying to define the other, would fail to be part of an integrated Christian life.

But Paul is speaking only of marriage; does this rule out other kinds of sexual partnership? Paul doesn't say so in quite so many words, but the implication is probably there (and most Christians have read him in this way). Perhaps we might see why such a conclusion could be drawn if we reflect on what he has said about this mutual yielding of power in marriage. All relations are in fact complicated by anxieties and unevennesses in the power and freedom of the partners. Can I trust enough to yield my liberty, to put my power and freedom at someone else's disposal, without covenant and promise, the tangible assurance that my giving is met by another's? Can I take this admittedly great risk without some way of knowing that the other isn't going to hold back and reserve their resources just in case I turn out not to be good enough, not to match their fancies or expectations? On the horizon is very definitely the idea that mutual yielding properly goes with mutual promise.

Something of this is also traceable in the last section of 1 Corinthians 6. Christians don't use prostitutes, because the exploitation of a prostitute involves the whole body of Christ. If I am involved in such a transaction, it affects all the relations in which I am involved as a member of the community of the Spirit. 'Your body is a temple of the Holy Spirit', says Paul; and that Spirit, as he explains again and again elsewhere, is the power by which Christians can live together without rivalry and selfishness, in a climate of mutual giving and receiving. An 'impersonal' sexual transaction poisons the *community's* life; it somehow affects everyone's integrity. So my policy about sexual behaviour isn't just my business: it is part of that vast and often obscure network that gives us our new being as Christians, our being-for-each-other in the Church. The community thus has an interest in what I decide about sex. Not a prurient and gossipy interest; and not that (God forbid) it should be instituting inquisitions into sexual behaviour; but it has a legitimate claim to put before believers their responsibility to the whole body, and thus to ask that sexual commitments be honestly open in the community, a proper public matter, supported by the community and in turn nourishing the life of the community. (It is one of the most painfully difficult aspects of the Church's traditional teaching on same-sex relationships that this openness has so often been made impossible; whatever view is taken of the need to rethink this area, the effect of much teaching has been to encourage a lack of honesty.)

These, then, are some of the clues Paul gives. He does not write a rule book, but sets an agenda. Later Christianity thought it better to write rules; it took these insights and set up a wide-ranging and sophisticated scheme of sexual law which eventually turned all this into something rather different. For Paul, the distinctively Christian meanings of sex are shown in relations of promise and constancy that allow us the freedom to be vulnerable. If we live our lives otherwise, we hurt the common life of the Church. But this is not quite the same as saying categorically that it is only in marriage that anything of these meanings comes to light, or that anything other than marriage is sin and nothing else. I can't see that the New Testament easily allows any *straightforwardly* positive evaluation of sexual intimacy outside a relationship that is publicly committed; but it does not suggest that the essential test of Christian orthodoxy lies in a willingness to treat *all* other relationships as totally incapable of sharing in the love of God. What we have is a focal and compelling set of images that can be translated into terms of behaviour by saying, 'Sexual intimacy is fully what it should be for Christians, a sign of God's vulnerable commitment, in *this* context of public promise and exclusive fidelity.' Claims for any other contexts would have to be argued hard – and the Church has seen no compelling reason for changing its mind about the primacy of 'covenanted' relationships. The fact that people learn, often by false starts, by giving and receiving hurts, with the best will in the world, by discovering their self-deceitfulness and so on, is another story, a story all too familiar to many of us; but something of God is discoverable even in what we may recognize as involving error. In many parts of the Church – notoriously – it looks as if the jury is still out on the question of whether some kinds of homosexual relation are effectively of the same kind as those relations between the sexes that Paul outlines, to the degree that this might outweigh Paul's denunciation of the prevailing homosexual lifestyles of his own day. These uncertainties are not going to disappear in a hurry – and, as I have hinted, it is very peculiar that attitudes to them should have become a touchstone of orthodoxy, in a way that the New Testament gives little support to. The main thing is to have our eyes firmly on what is central and distinctive in both Paul and Jesus: sex is not everything, and there are imperatives more urgent where the Kingdom of God is concerned; but sex is capable of revealing God in the deliberate weakness of a love that entrusts itself to another with no pre-negotiated limits of time and availability. That, says Scripture, is what sexual intimacy *can* be for humans. As so often with the New Testament, the question is thrown back to us: now what are you going to do about making such a possibility real?

PART THREE

PRAYER AND
CONTEMPLATION

7

CONTEMPLATION AND MISSION

'How good and how pleasant a thing it is when brethren dwell together in unity', says the psalmist. The gathering of bishops in Synod for the good of all Christ's people is one of those disciplines that sustain the health of Christ's Church. And today especially we cannot forget that extraordinary gathering of *fratres in unum* that was the Second Vatican Council, which did so much for the health of the Church and helped the Church to recover so much of the energy needed to proclaim the Good News of Jesus Christ effectively in our age. For so many of my own generation, even beyond the boundaries of the Roman Catholic Church, that Council was a sign of promise, a sign that the Church was *strong* enough to ask itself some demanding questions about whether its culture and structures were adequate to the task of sharing the Gospel with the complex, often rebellious, always restless mind of the modern world.

The Council was, in so many ways, a rediscovery of *evangelistic* concern and passion, focused not only on the renewal of the Church's own life but also on its credibility in the world. Texts such as *Lumen gentium* and *Gaudium et spes* laid out a fresh and joyful vision of how the unchanging reality of Christ living in his Body on earth through the gift of the Holy Spirit might speak in new words to the society of our age and even to those of other faiths. It is not surprising that we are still, 50 years later, struggling with many of the same questions and with the implications of the Council; and I take it that this Synod's concern with the new evangelisation is part of that continuing exploration of the Council's legacy.

But one of the most important aspects of the theology of the second Vaticanum was a renewal of Christian anthropology. In place of an often strained and artificial neo-scholastic account of how grace and nature were related in the constitution of human beings, the Council built on the greatest insights of a theology that had returned to earlier and richer sources – the theology of spiritual geniuses like Henri de Lubac, who reminded us of what it meant for early and mediaeval Christianity to speak of humanity as made in God's image, and of grace as perfecting and transfiguring that image so long overlaid by our habitual 'inhumanity'. In such a light, to proclaim the Gospel is to proclaim that it is at last possible to be properly human: the Catholic and Christian faith is a 'true humanism', to borrow a phrase from another genius of the last century, Jacques Maritain.

Yet de Lubac is clear what this does not mean. We do not *replace* the evangelistic task by a campaign of 'humanisation'. 'Humanize before Christianizing? If the enterprise succeeds, Christianity will come too late: its place will be taken. And who thinks that Christianity has no humanizing value?' So de Lubac writes in his wonderful collection of aphorisms, *Paradoxes of Faith.*[1] It is the faith itself that shapes the work of humanising and the humanising enterprise will be empty without the definition of humanity given in the Second Adam. Evangelisation, old or new, must be rooted in a profound confidence that we have a distinctive human destiny to show and share with the world. There are many ways of spelling this out, but in these brief remarks I want to concentrate on one aspect in particular.

To be fully human is to be recreated in the image of Christ's humanity; and that humanity is the perfect human 'translation' of the relationship of the eternal Son to the eternal Father, a relationship of loving and adoring self-giving, a pouring out of life towards the Other. Thus the humanity we are growing into in the Spirit, the humanity we seek to share with the world as the fruit of Christ's redeeming work, is a *contemplative* humanity. St Edith Stein observed that we begin to understand theology when we see God as the 'First Theologian', the first to speak about the reality of divine life, because 'all speaking about God presupposes God's own speaking'; in an analogous way we could say that we begin to understand contemplation when we see God as the first contemplative, the eternal paradigm of that selfless attention to the Other that brings not death but life to the self. All contemplating of God presupposes God's own absorbed and joyful knowing of himself and gazing upon himself in the trinitarian life.

To be contemplative as Christ is contemplative is to be open to all the fullness that the Father wishes to pour into our hearts. With our minds made still and ready to receive, with our self-generated fantasies about God and ourselves reduced to silence, we are at last at the point where we may begin to grow. And the face we need to show to our world is the face of a humanity in endless growth towards love, a humanity so delighted and engaged by the glory of what we look towards that we are prepared to embark on a journey without end to find our way more deeply into it, into the heart of the trinitarian life. St Paul speaks (II Cor. 3.18) of how 'with our unveiled faces reflecting the glory of the Lord', we are transfigured with a greater and greater radiance. That is the face we seek to show to our fellow human beings.

And we seek this not because we are in search of some private 'religious experience' that will make us feel secure or holy. We seek it because in this self-forgetting gazing towards the light of God in Christ we learn how to look at one another and at the whole of God's creation. In the early Church, there was a clear understanding that we needed to advance from the self-understanding or self-contemplation that taught us to discipline our greedy instincts and cravings to the 'natural contemplation' that perceived and venerated the wisdom of God in the order of the world and allowed us to see created reality for what it truly was in the sight of God – rather than what it was in terms of how we might use it or dominate it. And from there grace would lead us forward into true 'theology', the silent gazing upon God that is the goal of all our discipleship.

In this perspective, contemplation is very far from being just one kind of thing that Christians do: it is the key to prayer, liturgy, art and ethics, the key to the essence of a renewed humanity that is capable of seeing the world and other subjects in the world with freedom – freedom from self-oriented, acquisitive habits and the distorted understanding that comes from these. To put it boldly, contemplation is the only ultimate answer to the unreal and insane world that our financial systems and our advertising culture and our chaotic and unexamined emotions encourage us to inhabit. To learn contemplative practice is to learn what we need to live truthfully and honestly and lovingly. It is a deeply revolutionary matter.

In his autobiography,[2] Thomas Merton describes an experience not long after he had entered the monastery where he was to spend the rest of his life. He had contracted flu, and was confined to the infirmary for a few days, and, he says, he felt a 'secret joy' at the opportunity this gave him for prayer – and 'to do everything that I want to do, without having to run all over the place answering bells'. He is forced to recognise that this attitude reveals that 'All my bad habits ... had sneaked into the monastery with me and had received the religious vesture along with me: spiritual gluttony, spiritual sensuality, spiritual pride.' In other words, he is trying to live the Christian life with the emotional equipment of someone still deeply wedded to the search for individual satisfaction. It is a powerful warning: we have to be very careful in our evangelisation not simply to persuade people to apply to God and the life of the spirit all the longings for drama, excitement and self-congratulation that we so often indulge in our daily lives. It was expressed even more forcefully some decades ago by the American scholar of religion, Jacob Needleman, in a controversial and challenging book called *Lost Christianity*: the words of the Gospel, he says, are addressed to human beings who 'do not yet exist'.[3] That is to say, responding in a lifegiving way to what the Gospel requires of us means a transforming of our whole self, our feelings and thoughts and imaginings. To be converted to the faith does not mean simply acquiring a new set of beliefs, but becoming a new person, a person in communion with God and others through Jesus Christ.

Contemplation is an intrinsic element in this transforming process. To learn to look to God without regard to my own instant satisfaction, to learn to scrutinise and to relativise the cravings and fantasies that arise in me – this is to allow God to be God, and thus to allow the prayer of Christ, God's own relation to God, to come alive in me. Invoking the Holy Spirit is a matter of asking the third person of the Trinity to enter my spirit and bring the clarity I need to see where I am in slavery to cravings and fantasies, and to give me patience and stillness as God's light and love penetrate my inner life. Only as this begins to happen will I be delivered from treating the gifts of God as yet another set of things I may acquire to make me happy. And as this process unfolds, I become more free – to borrow a phrase of St Augustine (*Confessions* IV.7) – to 'love human beings in a human way', to love them not for what they may promise me, to love them not as if they were there to provide me with lasting safety and comfort, but as fragile fellow creatures held in the love of God. I discover (as we noted earlier) how to see other persons and things for what they are in relation to God, not to me. And it is here that true justice as well as true love has its roots.

The human face that Christians want to show to the world is a face marked by such justice and love, and thus a face formed by contemplation, by the disciplines of silence and the detaching of the self from the objects that enslave it and the unexamined instincts that can deceive it. If evangelisation is a matter of showing the world the 'unveiled' human face that reflects the face of the Son turned towards the Father, it must carry with it a serious commitment to promoting and nurturing such prayer and practice. It should not need saying that this is not at all to argue that 'internal' transformation is more important than action for justice; rather, it is to insist that the clarity and energy we need for doing justice requires us to make space for the truth, for God's reality to come through. Otherwise our search for justice or for peace becomes another exercise of human will, undermined by human self-deception. The two callings are inseparable, the calling to 'prayer and righteous action', as the Protestant martyr Dietrich Bonhoeffer put it, writing from his prison cell in 1944. True prayer purifies the motive, true justice is the necessary work of sharing and liberating in others the humanity we have discovered in our contemplative encounter.

Those who know little and care less about the institutions and hierarchies of the Church these days are often attracted and challenged by lives that exhibit something of this. It is the new and renewed religious communities that most effectively reach out to those who have never known belief or who have abandoned it as empty and stale. When the Christian history of our age is written – especially, though not only, as regards Europe and North America – we shall see how central and vital was the witness of places like Taizé or Bose, but also of more traditional communities that have become focal points for the exploration of a humanity broader and deeper than social habit encourages. And the great spiritual networks, Sant' Egidio, the Focolare, Communione e Liberazione, these too show the same phenomenon; they make space for a profounder human vision because in their various ways all of them offer a discipline of personal and common life that is about letting the reality of Jesus come alive in us.

And, as these examples show, the attraction and challenge we are talking about can generate commitments and enthusiasms across historic confessional lines. We have become used to talking about the imperative importance of 'spiritual ecumenism' these days; but this must not be a matter of somehow opposing the spiritual and the institutional, nor replacing specific commitments with a general sense of Christian fellow-feeling. If we have a robust and rich account of what the word 'spiritual' itself means, grounded in scriptural insights like those in the passages from II Corinthians that we noted earlier, we shall understand spiritual ecumenism as the shared search to nourish and sustain disciplines of contemplation in the hope of unveiling the face of the new humanity. And the more we keep apart from each other as Christians of different confessions, the less convincing that face will seem. I mentioned the Focolare movement a moment ago: you will recall that the basic imperative in the spirituality of Chiara Lubich was 'to make yourself one' – one with the crucified and abandoned Christ, one through him with the Father, one with all those called to this unity and so one with the deepest needs of the world. 'Those who live unity ... live by allowing themselves to penetrate always more into God. They grow always closer to God ... and the closer they get to him, the closer they get to the hearts of their brothers and sisters.'[4] The contemplative habit strips away an unthinking superiority towards other baptised believers and the assumption that I have nothing to learn from them. Insofar as the habit of contemplation helps us approach all experience as gift, we shall always be asking what it is that the brother or sister has to share with us – even the brother or sister who is in one way or another separated from us or from what we suppose to be the fullness of communion. *Quam bonum et quam jucundum* ... 'How good and pleasant a thing it is ...'

In practice, this might suggest that wherever initiatives are being taken to reach out in new ways to a lapsed Christian or post-Christian public, there should be serious work done on how such outreach can be grounded in some ecumenically shared contemplative practice. In addition to the striking way in which Taizé has developed an international liturgical 'culture' accessible to a great variety of people, a network like the World Community for Christian Meditation, with its strong Benedictine roots and affiliations, has opened up fresh possibilities here. What is more, this community has worked hard at making contemplative practice accessible to children and young people, and this needs the strongest possible encouragement. Having seen at first hand – in Anglican schools in Britain – how warmly young children can respond to the invitation offered by meditation in this tradition, I believe its potential for introducing young people to the depths of our faith to be very great indeed. And for those who have drifted away from the regular practice of sacramental faith, the rhythms and practices of Taizé or the WCCM are often a way back to this sacramental heart and hearth.

What people of all ages recognise in these practices is the possibility, quite simply, of living more humanly – living with less frantic acquisitiveness, living with space for stillness, living in the expectation of learning, and most of all, living with an awareness that there is a solid and durable *joy* to be discovered in the disciplines of

self-forgetfulness that is quite different from the gratification of this or that impulse of the moment. Unless
our evangelisation can open the door to all this, it will
run the risk of trying to sustain faith on the basis of an
un-transformed set of human habits – with the all too
familiar result that the Church comes to look unhap-
pily like so many purely human institutions, anxious,
busy, competitive and controlling. In a very important
sense, a true enterprise of evangelisation will always
be a re-evangelisation of ourselves as Christians also, a
rediscovery of why our faith is different, transfiguring, a
recovery of our own new humanity.

And of course it happens most effectively when we
are not planning or struggling for it. To turn to de Lubac
once again, 'He who will best answer the needs of his
time will be someone who will not have first sought
to answer them';[5] and 'The man who seeks sincerity,
instead of seeking truth in self-forgetfulness, is like
the man who seeks to be detached instead of laying
himself open in love.'[6] The enemy of all proclamation
of the Gospel is self-consciousness, and, by definition,
we cannot overcome this by being more self-conscious.
We have to return to St Paul and ask, 'Where are we
looking?' Do we look anxiously to the problems of our
day, the varieties of unfaithfulness or of threat to faith
and morals, the weakness of the institution? Or are we
seeking to look to Jesus, to the unveiled face of God's
image in the light of which we see the image further
reflected in ourselves and our neighbours?

That simply reminds us that evangelisation is always
an overflow of something else – the disciple's journey to
maturity in Christ, a journey not organised by the ambi-
tious ego but the result of the prompting and drawing of

the Spirit in us. In our considerations of how we are once again to make the Gospel of Christ compellingly attractive to men and women of our age, I hope we never lose sight of what makes it compelling to ourselves, to each one of us in our diverse ministries. So I wish you joy in these discussions – not simply clarity or effectiveness in planning, but joy in the promise of the vision of Christ's face, and in the foreshadowings of that fulfilment in the joy of communion with each other here and now.

8

ICONS AND THE PRACTICE OF PRAYER

Obviously, one of the first things that any visitor to an Orthodox church will notice is the devotion paid to icons. People make ritual prostration before them. They kiss them and light candles in front of them; and, as I'll explain a little further on, these icons have a role in certain sacramental actions as well.

This devotion is not a modern thing. So far as we can discern, it goes well back before the sixth century. And when the great controversy first arises in the seventh century over the use of icons in the Byzantine Empire, it is in terms not simply of the *theory* of icon painting but of the practice of devotion. Forms of honour paid to holy images – burning lights or incense in front of them, bowing to them – were associated by the iconoclasts with idolatry. But because the controversy was about practice as well as theory, the theological response to the anti-icon movement had to be elaborated in terms of the rationale of the practices of Christian people. In other words, the iconoclast controversy prompted the first really systematic treatment of what was supposed to be going on, in both the painting and the veneration of icons.

At the time, devotion to icons was seen by some as a sin inviting divine retribution. Why were the armies of Islam gaining so many victories? Well, the Muslims did not venerate images and the Byzantines did. There seemed to many to be a prima facie case that the wrath of God rested on the Byzantine armies because of their idolatry. But the price of all this was rapidly seen to involve the dismantling of a very complex theological synthesis achieved in the two centuries immediately before the controversy over the use of icons. And while the popularity in some areas of the anti-icon movement doubtless owed a good deal to the military successes of the iconoclast Emperor Leo, the deeply ingrained cultus eventually triumphed over more narrowly political considerations.

I want to explore a little why exactly the attack on icons was seen as the dissolution of a historic theological synthesis, and how the restoration and elaboration of that synthesis laid some of the foundations for the devotional use of icons in later centuries – and indeed the elaborations that continue to the present day in the use of icons as a means of prayer. The argument of those opposed to the veneration of icons – apart from the bald accusation of idolatry – boiled down to something like this: Jesus Christ is God incarnate; God is not capable of being represented. Either you then represent the humanity of Jesus alone, which is heretical because his humanity is never divorced from his divinity, or you purport to display his divinity, which is impossible – and heretical as well, in the sense that any claim to portray his divinity suggests a diminished and trivialised view of God. Therefore, the inexorable conclusion is that you cannot represent Christ truthfully.

This argument in itself takes a good deal for granted about the already current rhetoric of God being beyond all representation and God's essence or substance being beyond all concept, as well as appealing to the indivisibility of the human and the divine in Jesus. But the response of those who defended the cultus of icons was to draw on some of the theories elaborated particularly in the work of the greatest theologian of the seventh century, Maximus the Confessor.

Maximus, like other Greek theologians before and after him, argued that while we could not see or understand or apprehend the essence of God, we did encounter his action, his 'energy'. This, mediated and manifested in plural, interweaving forms, was what percolated through the entire material universe by virtue of the act of creation, and it was raised to a far higher power in the lives of holy people, and to a supreme state of unbroken intensity in the incarnate humanity of Jesus Christ. In other words, the relationship of the invisible, unknowable God to the material world, whether in Jesus Christ or more generally, was not simply the relationship of a self-enclosed divinity, infinitely distant from all material reality. It was the relationship of an active, outpouring, self-diffusing God whose action, you might say, soaked through the material environment, so that there was indeed a 'real presence' – and I use the words advisedly – of God within creation, and, by the work of grace and the Holy Spirit, an intensified presence of God in baptised people; even more intensified in those who took their baptism seriously and became saints; and supremely intensified in Jesus Christ.

So it's quite true that you can't represent God. But, for a theologian like Maximus, you are not trying to represent God as God 'in himself', which would be a nonsense or a blasphemy. When painting an icon, you seek to represent the way in which the divine energy is present in a material body or a material event in the history of God's dealings with the world. You are representing the lasting *effect* of God on and in the material world. So, in the case of Jesus, you are not trying to represent a humanity divorced from divinity, the humanity of Jesus 'alone'. Represent the humanity of Jesus and you represent a face, a body, a physique, permeated and animated uniquely with divine action. And so in the human and material reality of Jesus of Nazareth, human activity is shot through with divine activity. There is what Maximus and others called a 'theandric', a 'divine-human', reality going on there, and the icon, the image of Jesus Christ, represents that theandric reality – the interweaving (not fusion or confusion) of the endless divine resourcefulness of agency and love with the particularities of a human life.

The Seventh General Council, which pronounced in favour of the legitimacy of the cultus of icons, said of holy images in a very interesting phrase, 'They are in communion with him' (that is, with God). The image is *in communion* with what it represents. This is a very significant concept as we unpick the history and the practice of devotion to icons and their role in prayer across the centuries. It's put rather neatly by a contemporary iconographer and writer, Solrunn Nes, in her book on the iconography of the transfiguration in Orthodox art.[1] She discusses one particular image, the depiction of the patron saint in Sant' Apollinare in Classe in Ravenna, where the saint stands in the middle of a field full of lambs, gazing upwards towards a cross in heaven, before

which are three lambs, two on one side, one on the
other, which is generally held to be a symbolic representation of the transfigured Christ with the three apostles,
Peter, James and John, before his transfigured glory.
Solrunn Nes points out that St Apollinaris is standing in
the same field as the cross and the lambs; he is part of
the same landscape as the transfigured Christ, so that,
in terms of this representation, she says, Apollinaris 'is
what he is through his relationship with Christ'. So the
holy image in this context is the depiction not only of
Christ's divinely 'saturated' humanity, but also of other
humans in contact or communion with Christ, sharing
some measure of that saturation with divine energy,
divine activity. Just as when you depict Christ you depict
a humanity permeated with the divine action, so with
the holy person you depict someone who, in union or
communion with Jesus Christ by the power of the Spirit,
is likewise carrying, transmitting, divine agency, divine
light. And this means that even in narrative icons, icons
depicting a scene or a sequence of scenes, the figures you
see represented are not acting or operating in what you
might call a neutral space. This is not any old observer's snapshot of what certain people are doing. It is a
collection of people whose action together in this event
is given its meaning and coherence by its relation to the
action of God. This is why an Orthodox icon of the
Nativity is so strikingly different from the way you see
it depicted in the West. It is not the depiction of a scene
2,000 years ago in the Middle East, but an arrangement
of a whole series of figures who, in their different relations to the central figure of the Virgin and her child, are
in turn relating to God and moving towards the fullness
of their relation to him.

This is some of the theological background that had been elaborated during and after the controversy over icons in the seventh, eighth and ninth centuries, some of the thinking about the broad themes of theology and spirituality that informed the way in which the use of icons in public and private prayer came to be justified. And in the process of clarifying the legitimacy of venerating icons it was made very clear that what is venerated in the icon is not God as such, and therefore the 'worship' (to use what is in English a rather unhelpful word) given to icons is *not* what in Greek is called *latreia,* the devotion or submission given to God alone. It is *doulia,* service, reverence – short of what is due to God but appropriate to a human life or context in which the action of God is so (in every sense) materially present and at work: a reverence directed to the tangible *effect* of God, as I said earlier. And this means that the iconic representation of a saint is itself a representation of a person in prayer: whether literally or not depicting someone in the *act* of praying, it is always a depiction of someone whose prayerfulness relates them to God and whose meaning, whose identity, is finally provided in and through that relationship. It is a depiction of someone open to divine action and, as such, also capable of transmitting divine action.

So an icon shows you a relationship, but also begins to *enable* a relationship. Some of the most powerful, best-known and most ancient iconic forms and styles are, in fact, full-face representations of Christ, of Mary or of the saints, where the exaggeration of the size of the eyes – rooted in Egyptian coffin-painting styles of the late antique period – allows the intensity of gaze to become a means (once again) of communion. As some modern iconographers and commentators on iconography have observed, the icon itself thus becomes a kind of theological statement about what the grace of contemplative prayer and holy living entails. The icon declares that it is possible for human beings in communion with Christ to be bearers of divine action and divine light. I mention divine *light* specifically because this is a recurrent theme in Eastern Christian spirituality in the Middle Ages and afterwards; and increasingly it comes to be interwoven with both the thinking and the practice of icon painting. When the Orthodox believer begins morning prayer in front of the icon of Christ, he or she says this: 'Christ the true light, enlighten all who come into this world. Lift up the light of your face on us that in it we may behold the unapproachable light. Guide our footsteps in the path of your commandments through the prayers of your most pure Mother and of all the Saints.' You can see there the trace of the kind of theological vision that I mentioned earlier. 'The unapproachable light of God in himself' is 'refracted' through the human face of Christ upon us.

But the discussion of the divine light became, in the fourteenth century, a very embittered and complex subject in the Byzantine Empire. Controversies began among the monks of Mount Athos over the possibility of beholding God's light. Contemplatives on Mount Athos claimed that in advanced states of contemplation they beheld what they described as the 'uncreated' light, that is the eternal light of God's own presence, and that the purpose of contemplation was precisely to rise to that stage where they could see the light of their own minds in the light of God – and also that this was more than metaphorical language, that human eyes actually saw immaterial and eternal radiance. You will find a number of very interesting precursors of such language in spiritual writing as early as the turn of the fourth and fifth Christian centuries – the language of seeing your own light in the light of God, of perceiving the radiance of God with something analogous to physical sight. But it occasioned a great deal of controversy at the time, especially on the part of some in the Byzantine Empire influenced by Latin scholastic thought: uncreated light is *uncreated* light, they said, which means that by defi- nition created organs cannot see it. The claims of the contemplatives of Mount Athos were dismissed rather peremptorily by calling them *omphalopsychoi*, people who 'look for their souls in their navels' – referring to the practice among these contemplatives of saying their prayers bent almost double, their eyes focused on the lower chest.

However, a very elaborate and sophisticated defence was mounted by a number of theologians, includ- ing Gregory Palamas who became Archbishop of Thessalonica. He argued – very much along the lines that we have already summarised – that the light perceived by the contemplative in an advanced stage of prayer was of course the presence and effect of God's action – 'uncreated' in the sense that it sprang directly from the act of God and nothing else. But thus it is not a claim to see the *essence* or the nature of God in a literalist, mate- rialist way. Rather it is one example of how the divine energy communicates to the human self, to the *nous*, in Greek – a hard word to translate: 'intellect' is not very helpful, given its modern cerebral associations, and even 'spirit' gives slightly the wrong impression. 'Heart' or 'mind' is closer, so long as we forget the emotional resonances of the one and the rational resonances of the other. You could say, perhaps, that it is the *subject* oriented God-wards, exposed to the light of God, the effect of God's presence.

It is not by any means an accident that in the second half of the fourteenth century and through to the fifteenth century there are many instances of iconographers in Greece, in the Balkans and in Russia apparently giving far more sophisticated attention to the use of highlighting in icon-painting technique – as if part of the function of the icon now becomes much more obviously to depict something like the effect of divine light. There has always been in the tradition of icon production an interest in the source of light and the transmission of light in the composition, but if you look at some of the late-fourteenth and fifteenth-century icons from across the Byzantine world, you can see a quite remarkable intensity in the depiction of highlighting. The work of Theophanes or Feofan, the Greek iconographer who settled in Russia, which you can still see in Novgorod, is exceptional in this regard: the effect is to present you with an almost indistinguishably dark face (even allowing for the ravages of the centuries) with lightning streaks of white across it – cheekbones, noses and so forth shining almost with the effect of a photographic negative.[2] Feofan was in contact with the Athonite monks who were speculating about the divine light in contemplation, and it is not hard to see some carrying-over at this point of something of the theological and spiritual dispute into the actual business of painting.

All this reinforces the sense already present in the controversies of the seventh and eighth centuries that there is a connection between the state of the figure depicted in the icon and the potential state of someone praying in the presence of the icon. The person depicted is someone receptive to, saturated with, divine light and divine energy. The person praying exposes himself or herself to an action, and so to the possibility of transfiguration of the same kind. In other words, the person who stands in front of the icon is not the only one doing the looking. Such a person is *being seen*, being acted upon, in this framework. The icon, therefore, is not a passive bit of decoration but an active presence. And this means that both collectively and individually the icon depicts what the life of the baptised is about. Collectively, it means that the congregation meeting in a church decorated with icons is meeting in the presence of transfigured lives, the presence of holy people. Their prayer is actively associated with the prayer of all those depicted around them. It means the individual person praying, meditating in front of the icon, is similarly experiencing a share in the prayer of the person depicted – which perhaps makes some sense of why people may sometimes use language about icons as themselves 'interceding'. The icon is an 'intercessor', an active mediator, because it is a presence that draws you into a shared prayer. The praying individual associates himself or herself with the prayer of the figure depicted.

But the central significance here of what I've called 'being acted upon' and being looked at is consistently associated with the significance of the face and the eyes in the icon and the extreme rarity of any depiction of anyone in profile. Profile means a lack of communion or communication. The figure depicted in profile in the icon is not relating either to God or the beholder and is therefore someone you ought to look at rather suspiciously.

You will have endless examples of three-quarter portrayals, but strict *profiles* are rare. Demons appear in profile for the obvious reason that they have the strongest vested interest in preventing communion with anybody at all. And you will sometimes see what you might call 'neutral' figures depicted in profile – by which I mean figures who don't have a very marked role in the story. In the icon of the nativity, you will quite often see a stray shepherd chatting to Joseph in the corner, and this figure is quite regularly shown in profile, not because he is diabolical but simply because he doesn't actually matter a great deal in this event. Interestingly, in some icons of the resurrection, or more particularly the Harrowing of Hell where Christ descends to the Realm of the Dead and takes Adam in one hand and Eve in the other to draw them out of darkness, you'll see Adam depicted in profile, presumably because Adam is responsible for the first great decisive breach in communion between Heaven and Earth, and therefore he has a journey to undertake: his face has to be turned around, quite literally.

But to speak of this dimension of communion is also to be reminded of some of the liturgical functions of the icon. While icons are omnipresent in an Orthodox church it may seem at first as though they do not have very much immediate and direct liturgical use during, for example, a Eucharistic liturgy. This is true enough: they are greeted, honoured with incense at various points, but they do not seem to figure very much in how the actual shape of the liturgy unfolds. But to understand the potential of their role you have to turn to one or two other sacramental rites in the Orthodox Church. In the ordination of a deacon, for example, when the first examinations of the candidate for ordination have been concluded, the candidate for the diaconate moves to stand motionless in front of one of the icons on the screen until a much later stage in the liturgy where he is summoned back, hands are laid on him and, as a deacon, he goes to stand in front of the other icon. I'm talking here of the two icons of Our Lady and Christ flanking the Royal Doors in the centre of the icon screen. Thus the deacon in his ordination is being conformed to Mary and Jesus. And his growth into the 'bearing' of Christ, and his mediation of the service that Christ gives to the world, are signalled by these moves in the liturgy of ordination.

This is expressed even more explicitly in the Slavonic form of confession to a priest, where the rubric directs the priest to take the penitent before the icon of Christ on the doors of the icon screen with a prayer inviting the penitent to make confession including the phrase, 'His holy image is before us and I am only a witness, bearing testimony of those things which you tell me.' In this liturgical moment, the priest *steps back* to bring the penitent into communion with the Christ depicted in the holy image, since what happens in confession is first and foremost the searching of the heart by Christ rather than the examination by a priest.

This fits into an entire vision, an entire perspective on liturgy in the Eastern Church as an exposure to divine energy/divine action. We are brought back again to the 'hierarchy' of the intensity of the presence of divine action: the divine presence in the entire world symbolised by the very shape of the classical Byzantine church, the cross-in-square shape, which represents the Earth, the universal totality of the world; represented *then* by the symbolic presence of holy people in the icons; represented by the reality of the presence of Christ and the Spirit in the baptised community, and then, supremely, in the sacramental gift where the divine energy of the incarnate Christ is made directly available in the sanctified bread and wine. Thus the liturgical use and presence of icons is part of an entire understanding of the life of prayer, the baptised life, as being brought *into* a presence so as oneself to *become* a kind of presence.

A lot has been written about icons in the last few decades by Orthodox theologians and practitioners of iconography. In the last part of this reflection, I want to refer initially to the writings of one of the very great twentieth century iconographers, Leonid Ouspensky, who spent most of his working career in Paris, and left an extraordinary legacy of impressive and sophisticated work in a number of churches in France and elsewhere. But he also left a legacy of theological reflection on what he was essentially doing as a painter of icons. It's a reflection informed by a formidable theological learning. 'The icon,' Ouspensky writes:

> is both the way and the means. It is prayer itself.
> Hence its hieratic quality, its majestic simplicity
> and calmness of movement. Hence the rhythm of
> its lines, the rhythm and joyfulness of its colours
> which spring from perfection of inner high. A
> person's transfiguration communicates itself to all
> the surroundings for an attribute of holiness is a
> sanctification of all the surrounding world with
> which a saint comes into contact. Sanctity has not
> only a personal but also a general human as well as
> a cosmic significance. Therefore, all the visible world

represented in the icon changes, becomes the image of the future unity of the whole creation, the kingdom of the Holy Spirit.[3]

This powerful and poetic evocation of what a great iconographer thought he was doing draws together a great deal of what I've been trying to open up here. The icon is the way and the means. It *shows* what it sets out to *achieve*. It shows a transformed humanity radiant with a light not of this world. It aims to communicate that light to the beholder and make that light real in the beholder, as part of the whole process of exposure to the work of the Holy Spirit in the Church. What Ouspensky underlines, in a very telling way, is the rationale of what some people would call the 'non-realist' dimension of icon painting. Icons are not meant to be portraits in any sense. (There are some very interesting questions indeed as to how, in an age of photography, you paint adequate or appropriate icons of people whose actual historical appearance is well documented; the current development of a set of conventions for representing the twentieth-century martyr St Maria Skobtsova of Paris is a case in point.) They don't set out to be realistic depictions, either of the person or of the person's environment. The world in which figures are set in iconography is not a landscape in the ordinary sense. Ouspensky goes on to talk about the extraordinary things that some iconographers do with buildings in icons, discussing one Novgorod icon of the annunciation of the fifteenth century and observing how the background of buildings is actually worthy of a sort of Escher drawing, a complex of geometric impossibilities, and evidently deliberately conceived as such.[4] What you are invited to look at is not a person in a neutral field; you are invited to see the 'harmonics' of the new creation portrayed in visible form. And the connection of all this with the spiritual and theological synthesis out of which the defence of icons originally came is again worth noting.

We noted earlier the importance of Maximus the Confessor in the background of the history of thinking about icons. Maximus not only speaks about the divine energies penetrating the physical, he also speaks about the right and wrong use of images. By this he means primarily images of the mind – concepts, mental pictures, the whole routine activity of the mind in its imaginative capacity. He says very forcefully at one point that the purpose of self-denial and contemplation and prayer is *not* to get rid of beings and of images but to arrive at a state where the mind *perceives images without passion.*[5] 'Passion' is very much a technical term in this literature: it is the whole world of mutable, mobile, unreliable instinct and reaction, self-directed, ego-directed. The person praying or contemplating is on a journey that entails an 'excavation' of the passions and a disciplining of them. It is nothing to do with some sort of exclusion or denial of the emotions, but is about the rational inhabiting and understanding of the instinctual life in such a way that it doesn't take over and dictate your relations with God or with one another. The holy person is the one 'free from passion' because he or she is the person free from having their relations totally dictated by instinct, self-defence – reactivity, as we might say these days.

Maximus is not here writing primarily or specifically about visual images, but he is writing in a period where such images were available; and once again he is again giving a kind of theological clue which later generations – particularly in the last century or two – have willingly taken up. The figure depicted in the icon is not a figure designed to evoke in us *emotion* of the ordinary kind. Both the depiction and the effect are meant to take us beyond purely instinctual or reactive response. The icon, in other words, sets out to be the depiction of what Maximus and his generation would have called the *apathos* person, the person free from passion or instinct. And one of the things which twentieth century Eastern Christian commentators on aesthetics have often said is that there comes a point in Western religious art where it – disastrously – yields on this particular front: yields, that is, to the depiction of emotion and to a view of religious art as primarily about evoking appropriate emotions.

Those of you who know the Accademia in Venice will perhaps recall the strange experience of going from the fourteenth and fifteenth century rooms through to the eighteenth century and watching what happens to religious art in Venice during that period. It's an instructive journey to take, and rather bears out what our Eastern commentators have said. It is perfectly clear that during this period the priority of depicting and evoking appropriate emotion comes to control religious representation. And the icon in its classical form is meant not to address the emotion but to show passion transfigured or held in relation to God in such a way that it doesn't interfere with freedom, spiritual freedom. In such a way it is part of the whole dispensation by which grace is transmitted to the praying person so as to generate the same kind of transfiguration of the passions that holy people experience on the way to that final condition of contemplative liberty where the world of instinct and reaction is, for all practical purposes, done away with.

So when Ouspensky writes about our projection into the kingdom of the Spirit, he is drawing attention to that dimension of the icon which pushes beyond the emotional level, which takes us outside an aesthetic whose concern is primarily to show accurately how people are feeling so you may feel the same thing. It's one reason of course, why, in the early twentieth century, modernist artists in Russia were so fascinated by the icon and so often reverted to its conventions, its colour patterns and its linearity as a way of exploring their own agenda. I mentioned very briefly the question of colour, and several more lectures would be needed to unscramble some of the symbolic importance of the balance of colours in the history of icons (very much developed in a particular kind of Russian aesthetic at the end of the nineteenth century but not wholly absent in earlier centuries). It is perhaps worth noting a tanta- lising phrase from an early Christian writer of the fifth century, Diadochos of Photiki, who speaks[6] of how the work of redemption is rather like the work of an artist. First, you sketch in the outline in pencil, and then you put in the colours. So first, the Holy Spirit in baptism sketches out the 'outline' of Christ, into which you are going to move and in which you will live; and then the work of the Spirit as you grow in your discipleship fills in the colours. It is doubtful whether Diadochos could have been thinking specifically of the Christian artist or how many iconic depictions or iconographers he would have been familiar with at this early date. But it is one of those curious little elements of traditional perception which seems to contain in embryo many of the deeper themes that will unfold in the history of devotion and practice.

In summary, what I have been attempting to do is to locate the devotional practice around icons, early and contemporary, in the theological context in which it first developed and flourished; to try and show how the defence of icons in the context of the iconoclast controversy itself drew upon an immensely complex and sophisticated theological background; and how, in making that defence, it developed the theme still further. I have suggested some of the ways in which the spiritual controversies of the fourteenth century are again echoed in the practice of iconography, and how they contribute to our understanding of the overall framework. And I have hinted at some of the ways in which the presence of the icon in the liturgy is both an illustration and an intensification of what the liturgy itself as a whole is meant to be about. In the most general terms, we can say that the icon, from very early on, is conceived as one of the means of grace, one of the means of spiritual transformation, *representing what it is meant to effect*. Without an understanding of that context, that purpose – the icon as a means of spiritual transformation – holy images in the Eastern Christian tradition will make very much less sense. One may or may not approach them with an awareness of this theological and spiritual world. But to see the fullness and the richness of the thought that has nurtured them, the world of Christology and reflection on the contemplative task, is to be freed for a much fuller and more adequate response to their beauty.

PART FOUR

THE GENIUS OF TERESA
OF AVILA

9

What St Teresa Means to Me

I first read Teresa's autobiography as a teenager, and was both deeply engaged by it and deeply bewildered by how to understand my own life and prayer in the light of it. In the years that followed, it was John of the Cross who made more sense, I think because he offered a pattern of Christian growth that was very deliberately shaped by the model of Christ's self-emptying, and worked out in detail. But then in my thirties I returned to Teresa, when I was teaching a course on the Spanish contemplatives at Oxford, and realised a couple of things I had missed, with a lot of help from far better readers of Teresa such as Ruth Burrows (a really decisive influence in my Christian life) and Noel Dermot O'Donoghue, and with a growing awareness of the various embodiments of the Teresian ideal in those extraordinary Carmelite giants like Thérèse of Lisieux and Edith Stein (whose full intellectual as well as spiritual stature is hard to overstate). The things that came home to me included, above all, Teresa's passionate focus on the Incarnate Jesus, and her near-obsessive concern to eradicate considerations of social and racial distinction from her communities. I began to see her as a genuinely incarnational theologian; and I was more and more intrigued by the way in which her writing so skilfully negotiates the problems of being a woman – and an ethnically Jewish woman – in a pretty paranoid environment in which she would have been automatically suspect of all kinds of irregularity. Her courage and realism became more and more vivid to me, and the connection she consistently makes between the Incarnation and the radically simple and egalitarian style of life she insisted on in her communities seemed to me to be more and more obviously contemporary in its importance.

As I read her, she is saying first of all that Christ has made the way open for the Father to reach right into the depths of who we are, to reconnect with the buried image of God in us at our centre and lead it to full liberation. Contemplation is how we collaborate in this clearing of the way, leaving the space for God within and God beyond to meet. But this depends on the Son of God's work in making us his brothers and sisters; and Teresa's meditations on the Gospels' stories seem increasingly important to me as I re-read her. Jesus's accessibility to all is a constant theme, as is the wonder with which we should think about our inclusion in the family of Christ's brothers and sisters. His readiness to be in the company of any human being, of any background or race or status, makes the connection between a Christ who reaches out to the marginal and lost, and a life of religious contemplation which is in so many ways 'marginal' to the busy and anxious life of the religious institution. So this leads on directly to the need for a form of religious life that is stripped down, 'businesslike' in its simplicity, asking all to be involved with the most prosaic of tasks. What Teresa envisages for her communities, male and female, is a genuinely apostolic plainness. And she sees this as the most effective response we can make to a situation of deep crisis in the Christian world.

In all these ways, she seems to me to be a sharply and challengingly contemporary figure for us. Our Christian practice is fundamentally about nothing else than the re-creation in us of the divine image: Christ being shaped in our human lives. And so the work of contemplation is not a private specialism; if it is to do with our re-creation in the likeness of Jesus, it is at the very foundation of how we imagine our lives together as human beings. Our dignity depends not on our achievement or standing but on the decision of God in Christ to receive us as Christ's kindred. And if we are troubled by the conflicts and failures of the Church in our world, what we need to do is not to panic, or to freeze in defensive and angry posturing, but to get on with the real work of opening the way for God's transforming presence.

Teresa's incarnationalism is in essence – not surprisingly – close to John of the Cross's theology. But where he emphasises the way in which we participate in Christ's inner anguish as he is 'annihilated' in the desolation he endures on the cross, Teresa focuses more closely on the act of Christ's identifying with and reaching out to those who need his presence. If we wanted to put it neatly, we could say that John is concerned with how we identify with Christ through our own acceptance of inner desolation and loss, and Teresa is interested in how Christ identifies with us through his acceptance of the human condition, and how he thereby bestows dignity and worth on all. Only a very blinkered theology would see any contradiction here. But Teresa's own barbed comment on John – that he risked giving the impression that you needed to go through the intensities of the dark night before you could encounter Jesus fully – is a necessary reminder that all encounter with Jesus begins in his own reaching out to us. Whether she is right or wrong about John (and I think she is a bit unfair, if you read John's *Romanzas*, for example), Teresa is robustly defending the pattern set out in the Gospels, of a Christ who is always taking the first steps towards people. I have become fascinated recently by her use of the Gospel stories to underline this insight – how she is especially fond of the narratives of St Luke's Gospel in this respect. Taking for granted the mediaeval identification of Mary Magdalene, Mary of Bethany and the sinful woman at the house of Simon the Pharisee (an identification no longer accepted, of course), she builds up a sort of composite portrait of the contemplative who is also an outsider, a needy and fragile figure, not at the centre of society: for Teresa, the contemplative must have this as the model – the person who knows her need and her marginality, who opens up to the promise of encounter with Jesus and takes the risk of going on being an 'unprofitable' and embarrassing presence, shaping her life around sitting and listening to Jesus. Biblical scholarship may have rendered the assimilation of these New Testament figures no longer credible; but Teresa's 'composite portrait' still has its own power and integrity.

She is also a theologian of the Eucharist, for whom the sacrament extends this Gospel reality of Christ reaching out to the needy in our own daily experience. Christ's presence in the Mass is the tangible token of God's unchanging willingness to be with us in Christ. And in one tantalising meditation, Teresa pictures receiving Communion as a moment when Christ comes to the

Father who dwells in the depths of the soul, waiting for him – a singularly haunting, unusual and beautiful image.

Teresa has been precious to me as a writer who consistently makes it possible to connect contemplation with Scripture, with the sacramental life and with the witness of the Church in the world. For me, the essence of the contemplative life, whether lived in religious communities or not, is the realisation of the apostolic calling to be with Jesus as selflessly as possible – in the knowledge that the degree to which we stay in his company is the degree to which we make the right kind of difference in the world. In 2015 I found myself being asked to speak several times on both Teresa's 500th anniversary and the centenary of Thomas Merton's birth; and I have increasingly been drawn to speak about them together. They are dramatically different people, and I don't want to minimise the differences in style and personality, even sometimes in teaching. But what they do surely have in common is the conviction that contemplative life is central to the well-being and integrity of the Church, simply because it is the primary way in which we let ourselves as a Christian community make space for God to be God; and nothing could be more evidently good news for our world than the truth that God is God. The Gospel word is that God is faithful to what he has promised, and that what he has promised is his eternal friendship (a key category for Teresa) – and not only friendship but adoption into his own life. God is not only faithful, we might say – he is *faithfulness* in his very essence, the 'faithfulness' of the persons of the Holy Trinity to one another, the faithfulness of creator to creation and of Christ to his brothers and sisters.

The contemplative gaze into this mystery, lived out in a wondering love towards each other in the human world, releases us from anxiety and suspicion towards each other – and even towards God. It is because of this beautiful interweaving of themes, too often held apart, that Teresa's life and teaching have been and still are for me one of the greatest testimonies to that vision of the 'Godness' of God as made tangible in Jesus.

The two essays which follow this sketch of Teresa's significance are attempts to fill out the themes mentioned here, to do with her reading of the Gospels and her Eucharistic devotion.

10

TERESA AND THE SCRIPTURES

For a sixteenth-century nun, access to the text of Scripture would almost certainly have been restricted for the most part to what was available in liturgical books; nuns were not professional commentators on Scripture, as were those engaged in university teaching or canonical processes of formation for male clergy and religious, and only those employed in this context would have habitually used full texts of the Bible. A very brief glance at St John of the Cross's pattern of biblical citation will illustrate the point: John draws from a wide range of Old Testament books, including most of the prophets, and quotes verbatim, often quite copiously. The same holds for Francisco de Osuna's biblical references, though he has rather fewer word-for-word citations. By contrast, it is not surprising that, when Teresa refers to texts from Hebrew Scripture, they are usually paraphrased and come from a relatively narrow range of books:[1] the Psalms are of course the best represented book, followed by the Song of Songs, but apart from these, the majority of references are to fairly well-known incidents (the Burning Bush of Exodus 3, the crossing of the Red Sea, events in the life of Elijah), with a scattering of prophetic texts, all but one (an allusion in *Way of Perfection* 42.3 to Malachi 3.20, undoubtedly derived from a liturgical source, as it simply mentions the image of Christ as 'Sun of Righteousness') to Isaiah and Ezekiel. Job (quite frequently quoted by John of the Cross) appears a few times, reflecting probably the regular homiletic use of his story; there is only one actual quotation. The pattern of reference is exactly what we would expect from someone with no access to a complete vernacular Bible, accustomed to pick up phrases and narratives from liturgical and devotional/ homiletical contexts. Interestingly, Teresa refers in chapter 16.11 of the Way to 'reading the Passion' in a way which might suggest that this is a personal devotional activity as well as a liturgical observance. And this liturgical background to the use of texts makes sense of the pattern of Teresa's habits of allusion to the New Testament as well – most notably in the absence of anything reliably identifiable as an independent citation of Mark's Gospel: although the biblical indices to the standard editions and translations (including those in the Institute of Carmelite Studies translations) include putative references to Mark, the texts in question are all paralleled in Matthew or Luke, and it is very unlikely indeed that Teresa derived anything directly from a Gospel that was barely visible in liturgical usage, since it was generally regarded as an epitome of Matthew.

However, Teresa does undoubtedly cite Gospel texts with some regularity; and it is instructive to see exactly which she utilises most, and what picture they help to form of her own sense of where she saw herself and the vocation of her sisters in the Gospel framework. In the brief survey offered here, it will be clear that she has strong preferences in her habits of quotation, and that these sketch a distinctive biblical theology of the contemplative calling. For reasons that will emerge, she tends to use Lukan parables and narrative passages, although in strict quantitative terms it is Matthew that she quotes most often (over 50 times in the *Life*, the *Way* and the *Castle* all together). The Fourth Gospel is cited over 20 times in *The Interior Castle*, but is used a good deal less frequently in *The Way of Perfection* (11 times) and the *Life* (six times). As we shall see, quotations and allusions fall into 'clusters' – groups of texts regularly associated in Teresa's mind – and these give us our best clues as to how Teresa sought to deploy Gospel citation and allusion to illuminate the essentials of the Carmelite life. Thus in what follows, I have not tried to give a complete catalogue of all her Gospel references, but only to pick out the most frequent and telling concentrations of textual and narrative reference, to draw into better focus the theological priorities she brings to bear on her reading of the Gospels.

The Way of Perfection gives us the context in which she is working.[2] In the wake of the Inquisition's unprecedentedly severe restrictions (in the Index of 1559) on spiritual literature in the vernacular, the challenge for a community of laywomen unversed in Latin was a serious one. Teresa, in her *Life* (26.5) as well as – by implication – in *The Way of Perfection* (e.g. 21.3, with its reference to the books that cannot be taken away), laments the way in which communities like hers are deprived of theological and spiritual sustenance; but her response is to insist that all that is necessary can be drawn out of the texts that everyone knows and habitually uses – the Our Father and the Hail Mary – and from 'the words of the Gospels' (*Way of Perfection* 21.3). Books can indeed be dangerous and distracting, she disarmingly admits, but the text of the Gospels and of the familiar prayers, properly understood, will lead to recollection and interior prayer. Teresa claims (ibid.) that she has no intention of writing 'commentary' on the prayers; she is careful to use vocabulary which makes it plain that she is not setting herself up in the kind of role restricted to ordained males. All she intends is to persuade her sisters to go forward in the way of prayer, whatever risks there may seem to be, since in her view the life of the sisters in her communities is a necessary witness and reparation in an age of violent religious conflict and the widespread rejection (as she sees it) of sacramental life and devotion by the merging churches of the Reformation – 'Lutherans', as she characterises them all with a fine indiscriminate hostility. This life *needs* to be lived in the Church at such a period, and so there is need for a resource that will enable it to be lived with intelligence and integrity (see especially *Way* 1.2–5). Later on (37.1), she describes the Our Father as an 'evangelical' prayer – meaning, it seems, not just that it is literally found in the Gospels but that it can act as a summary of the Gospel itself. So her aim in the *Way* is to clarify the ground and trajectory of contemplative prayer with reference to nothing but what the layperson might know and hear or read. This provides a 'living book' (*Life* 26.5) where Christ speaks directly; and it is part of the process by which the community itself becomes a 'text' to communicate to the world God's promise and purpose at a time when – as she has spelled out at the beginning of the *Way* – the world is racked by religious confusion and rebellion.

As we have already noted, Matthew is her most frequent source for Gospel citations; only in the *Castle* do quotations from John outnumber those from Matthew. In the *Way*, Matthew is cited 22 times altogether; and the most pronounced 'cluster' of references is from the Sermon on the Mount – Jesus's commendation of prayer in solitude (Mt. 6.6) and the clauses of the Lord's Prayer. Elsewhere we find allusions to Matthew 11 ('Come to me all you who are weary and burdened...') in the *Life* (11.16), the *Soliloquies* (VIII.2) and possibly the *Way* (19.15), though this sounds more like John 7.37, 'Let anyone who is thirsty come to me and drink', recast in a slightly Matthaean form – as the same text is also in *Soliloquies* IX. Jesus's prayer in Gethsemane from Matthew 26 is referred to twice in the *Way* (30.2 and 32.6), to alert us to what is implied in praying 'Thy will be done', and is also referenced in *Meditations on the Song of Songs* 3.11; the *Castle* 2.11 alludes to the same episode in Gethsemane, but with reference to Jesus's injunction to the disciples to pray not to be brought into temptation. The *Way* 18.6 (possibly also 34.10) and the *Castle* 2.8 and 6.11 refer to the request of James and John to sit on either side of Jesus in the Kingdom (Mt. 20.22), and Jesus's reproach to them because they have not counted the cost of what they pray for.

These are the most significant allusions to Matthew's text – significant in the sense that they appear more than once in important contexts to make important points. Teresa's exegesis of the Lord's Prayer sets out the rationale for her insistence that the community must disregard considerations of social or ethnic status in their common kinship as adopted brothers and sisters of the eternal Son, sharing with him the liberty of approaching the Father (see particularly 27.6); her use of Christ's invitation ('Come to me all you who are weary...') underlines the priority of Christ's action in leading us into this adoptive relationship; and the references to the prayer in Gethsemane and the appeal of the sons of Zebedee warn of the cost of the contemplative life as a sharing in Christ's own bearing of the cross. Her quotation of Johannine texts comes at the basic theme of sharing Christ's intimacy with the Father by a slightly different route. Here, the most noticeable concentrations of reference – apart from allusions to the conversation with the Samaritan woman in John 4, to which we shall be returning – are to chapters 14, 17 and 20. The *Castle* has five references to John 14, one (1.1) to Christ's description of the place to which he goes as having 'many rooms' or 'many dwelling places' (Jn. 14.2, also referred to in *Way* 20.1 and *Life* 13.13), the others to later verses touching on Jesus as the way to the Father and on the Father as 'seen' in Jesus: and there are also four references to Jn. 17.20–23, on the mutual indwelling of Father and Son and their indwelling in the community of the faithful. Especially in *Castle* 7.7–9, this indwelling is understood as the goal of our own journey towards the centre of ourselves, where Son and Father 'encounter' each other in the created soul (c.f. no. 52 of the *Spiritual Testimonies*). In short, the citations of Matthew and John by Teresa are predominantly to do with emphasising that the relation between Christ and the Father as shown and enacted in the Gospel narrative is the form of our own relation to Christ's Father; and that this implies both the risk of following in the way of the cross and the radical spiritual/communal egalitarianism of a community united simply by the invitation of Christ.

When we turn to Teresa's use of Luke's Gospel, there is a noticeable shift of focus, although there are important

continuities with the themes so far outlined. The frequency
of Lucan material overall is not far short of her use of
Matthew (indeed, in the *Castle* Luke is slightly more
often quoted than Matthew, 16 as opposed to 15 times,
where John is quoted 25 times in all), and it is strongly
focused on specific *narratives* (including parables) rather
than teaching passages. It is also worth noting that her
Lukan citations have very limited overlap with those to
be found in John of the Cross or Osuna, who does not
refer to Teresa's two favourite texts, the Mary and Martha
story and the incident at the house of Simon the Pharisee
involving a 'sinful woman', though he does, like Teresa,
make use of the Lukan parables, notably the Prodigal
Son (*Abecedario* 1.1, 4.1, 13.2) and the Pharisee and the
Publican (8.1). Teresa's favoured narratives are regularly
about Jesus's relation to women followers and about
God's acceptance of sinners. The Mary and Martha story
from Luke 10 is the most frequently quoted (seven times
overall, four of these in the *Way*, two in the *Castle*, one in
the *Soliloquies*), followed closely by the story of the sinful
and penitent woman (Lk. 7) who anoints the feet of Jesus
when he visits the house of Simon the Pharisee (five references, two in the *Way*, three in the *Castle*). In addition
to this, we have mention of the parables of the Prodigal
Son and the Pharisee and the Tax-Collector (Lk. 15 and
18), the woman who touches the hem of Jesus's garment
(Lk. 8), and the penitent thief on the cross (Lk. 23).
Twice (*Way* 42.1, *Castle* 5.2.13) there is a quotation of
Luke 22.15 ('I have eagerly desired to eat this Passover
with you'): Jesus longs to be released from the sufferings
of this world, praying like us to be 'delivered from evil';
he responds just as any spiritually sensitive person must,
says Teresa in the *Way*. But in the *Castle*, she deploys this

differently in order to underline what must have been the strength of Jesus's desire to save our souls if it could overcome the natural fear and shrinking from profound pain and death.

One of the governing themes of this array of Lukan texts is thus Jesus's welcome of and passion for the sinner. But there is a more complex subtext to Teresa's citations. As we have noted, it is an obvious enough point about Teresa's rhetoric that she has to insist that she is not trying to 'teach' about the life of prayer, being a woman and therefore unqualified to do so; yet she cannot resist reminding her readers that Christ 'found as much love and more faith' in women as opposed to men, and that every virtue in women is automatically suspected by men (*Way* 3.7). Women are 'intimidated', she says, in this world; but they may still pray that God will allow them to receive the good things merited by the prayers of the Virgin, recalling that Christ invariably met women with compassion. Behind Teresa's exegesis of a specific passage lies this conviction, that the status accorded to women, especially women contemplatives, is at odds with the Gospel record in essential respects; and so she is especially concerned to make use of Gospel texts which make the point. Luke is uniquely well provided with these; but it is not surprising that she uses the Samaritan woman from John 4 in much the same way (three times in the *Way*, once in the *Castle*). Famously, in the *Vejamen*, her comments on the responses of various clerical associates to the words 'Seek yourself in me', she implicitly reproaches John of the Cross for implying that no-one can approach Christ without prior self-emptying and purification: 'The Magdalene was not dead to the world when she found him, nor was the Samaritan woman or the Canaanite woman' (pp. 360–1 in Volume III of the ICS translation; the Canaanite woman of Matthew 15 is cited more indirectly in *Foundations* 8.2, but is absent from other works). Jesus regards women without that 'suspicion' that is shown by the 'sons of Adam' (*Way*, 3.7). And what is more, he can be relied upon to *defend* the female contemplatives for whom Teresa writes.

This is one of the more distinctive arguments in Teresa's work. Like practically all her Catholic contemporaries, she assumes that the sinful woman at the house of Simon is identical not only with Mary of Bethany, Martha's sister, but with Mary Magdalene; and this enables her to present a figure whose relation to Jesus is repeatedly characterised by risk or scandal, *from which Jesus protects her.* So in chapter 15 of the *Way*, Teresa discusses how the sisters should react to criticism and blame, and prays in aid of Christ's defence of 'Magdalene' both from Simon the Pharisee and from her sister. This is at first sight simply about dealing with unmerited criticism as an individual; but when the theme recurs in chapter 17, the emphasis has moved somewhat. Mary is being criticised *for being a contemplative*: so the contemplative must be silent, waiting for Jesus to defend her. And Teresa, characteristically, adds that it will not do for the contemplative to look down on those who perform necessary practical tasks, since there are diverse callings at diverse moments, depending on the divine will (17.6–7). The *Castle's* 7.4.13 imagines 'Magdalene' abandoning her dignity and social status to go and perform a menial task for Jesus (washing his feet), living through a very public change of behaviour (and 'dress and everything else'), so that her contemplative life is grounded in the visible sacrifice of reputation and dignity that takes her to the feet of the Lord in action as well as contemplation (and prepares her for the dreadful suffering of witnessing Christ's crucifixion). Already in 6.11.12 of the *Castle*, Teresa has promised her sisters that Jesus will answer for them 'as he did for the Magdalene' when the intensity of spiritual longing brings about extreme conditions or behaviours. And all of this suggests that the discussion in *Way* 15 is not only about individual faults in the course of the common life, but also about the sense that the contemplative life itself is in some sense 'scandalous'.

In the context especially of the *Way*, this is a signifi-cant complex of ideas. We know that Teresa begins this work by articulating the insecurity of her position as a woman obliged by circumstance to provide some kind of spiritual formation for contemplatives who are not liter-ate in Latin, and who are in any case widely regarded as incapable of contemplation because of their sex. As she says, what would otherwise be called good is suspect in a woman; the contemplative calling is regarded as a matter of danger for a woman, and thus also for the Church as a whole, and the female contemplative becomes a 'transgressive' figure, rebelling against her role and status (or lack of status). In Teresa's environ-ment, the role of the female religious house was closely bound to a set of concerns about status. A little later, the Counter-Reformation was to intensify restrictions on female enclosure as an aspect of its interest in consolidat-ing the discipline and uniform behaviour of consecrated persons, priests, brothers and religious sisters; but this has not yet, in Teresa's day, become the issue it would be by the last quarter of the century. Teresa's problem is that the typical women's religious house of her era was – as so much of Teresa's correspondence and comments in the *Way* and the *Foundations* confirms – an institution that offered a clear 'contract' to its secular environment in terms of intercession, public recognition of patronage and reinforcement of family solidarity and dignity by provision for the unmarried without loss of standing.[3] It would be extreme to say that a distinctive theology of contemplative vocation for women was absent from the Church's vocabulary; but the intense suspicion directed at anyone who might be regarded as a *beata*, an unauthorised female religious teacher, meant that the spiritual expectations of a female religious had to be modest.[4] Claims about a calling to interior prayer, 'mental' prayer, had about them, in the ears of clerical authority, especially in Spain, an unacceptable flavour of appeal to a realm outside the mediations of grace in the life of the Church, grace as administered by a visibly authorised system of sacramental and doctrinal discipline. And a community that – like Teresa's – refused the 'contract' of local usefulness, declining the usual forms of patronage and so threatening to be a financial burden on top of all its other ambivalent features, was manifestly a problem: Teresa's frequently declared hostility to large-scale benefactions with strings attached meant that the financial situation of her houses was unusual, creating difficulties for local administrators, secular and religious.

All this is fairly familiar as a characterisation of what Teresa faced; but what makes her so theologically interesting in this context is precisely what she does with the common and authorised currency of liturgical prayer and scriptural narrative, to create a rationale for both the contemplative calling as such, and her own particular version of it as involving certain standards of simplicity and financial quasi-independence. If our reading of her practice as an interpreter of the Gospels is accurate, she is constructing just that theology of the contemplative calling – especially for women – that was occluded or discouraged in much of current teaching. Thus she lays general foundations in her meditations on the Our Father and related texts from Matthew, where, as we have seen, she first elaborates her convictions about how kinship with Christ relativizes other kinship claims; then emphasises the priority of Christ's call, and finally insists on the costliness of following this call.

This is further refined in her use of John's Gospel, in particular the Farewell Discourses: here the emphasis is on the abiding presence within the contemplative of the Trinitarian life, and the reality of the promised indwelling of Christ – with also a recognition (through the use of the 'many dwelling places' passage of Jn. 14.2) of the need for the soul to advance through a series of such 'dwelling places', the rooms of the interior castle, and also of the diversity of routes by which the soul moves God-wards, so that no soul with genuine desire for union with God is excluded, even if they are not in the conventional sense contemplatives.

And when Teresa turns to her Lukan material, this last point is given a further and potentially radical refinement. The general affirmation of diversities of calling turns into an affirmation of diversities that will appear problematic to some authorities: specifically, the calling of women to be both contemplative and active in the way they were meant to be in the reformed Carmels of Teresa's foundation is grounded in Jesus's

142

own affirmation of women who resisted convention in order to be in direct contact with him, both in practical service and in contemplative listening. Teresa does not set out to negate the hierarchical order in which she finds herself, but in effect challenges that order to recognise what the Christ of the Gospel narratives recognises: that women may be invited to the spiritual intimacy with him that is fulfilled in contemplation within an apostolic community. When, in *Way* 27.6, she apostrophises the 'college of Christ, where St Peter, being a fisherman, had more authority ... than St Bartholomew, who was a king's son', she is underlining the fact that the original apostolic community represented a refusal of pre-existing kinship and status patterns: thus, when contemporary women embark on journeys that appear as scandalous as that of 'Magdalene' to the house of Simon the Pharisee, we must see it in the context of that primitive refusal. The Carmelite calling may be suspect in the eyes of the current ecclesiastical world, but its advocate is Jesus himself.

Contemplation – especially in its 'Teresian' manifestation, accompanied by poverty and the repudiation of what I earlier called the 'contract' around religious life – becomes in this framework a place of 'otherness' in regard to the social order and its ecclesiastical reflections and accommodations. And it is even more confusing for the critic to the extent that Teresa refuses to settle with a clear traditional hierarchy of contemplative and active; what she has to say about this is often unclear, but what is plain is her unease with any typology that re-inscribes in the community a difference between high and low status. Thus in one of the passages where she addresses this (*Way* 17), she begins by reflecting on aspiration to contemplative prayer as an offence against humility: contemplation is precisely what cannot be planned or earned by human excellence, so we should not be seeking contemplative gifts as a way to reinforce our self-opinion. 'Not because all in this house practise prayer must all be contemplatives: that's impossible' (17.2). The life as a whole, the life of *all* in the community, has as its rationale the nurture of proper response to contemplative gifts from God. And one 'proper' response to these gifts in others is to accept that they are not, or not yet, for oneself. It is again a 'proper' response to assume that the lack of such gifts is caused by one's own failings (17.4), but equally proper not to conclude that one is fixed in inferiority: God requires all kinds of service. So if the gifts of mental prayer are not forthcoming, we do not despair but assume that the Lord is working with us in the way best suited to us at this particular moment. With a very Teresian touch she adds, 'I don't say that we shouldn't try' (17.7): contemplation is what we can rightly pray for, it seems, and it seems to be given when we are detached from any issues of status or success around it. The point is that the entire scheme of community life is both designed to pave the way for contemplative union *and* designed to make sense of the absence or delay of contemplative gifts, in the light of a strong belief in the dignity of any and every task performed in the convent for the service of Christ. Our individual spiritual growth is woven into the complex of tasks that make the community work; and one of the central paradoxes of this is the implied notion that 'active' service is justified by what it makes possible for the contemplative. Its 'usefulness' is to do with creating the ambience in which the 'useless' loving contemplation of God in Christ may flourish, whether in myself or in my neighbour.

Action is useful insofar as it allows uselessness; the disciplined life of the convent is not 'useful' because it guarantees prayerful support for kindred or city (not that these are in any way simply denied or disallowed by Teresa), but because it creates the environment in which something that is an end in itself, something that is not useful in terms of anything but itself, is made more attainable, at least for some. Precisely by withdrawing attention and attachment from the various kinds of social solidarity available outside the community – the solidarities of actual family relationships, the reinforcing of status and influence by conspicuous patronage – the community's discipline nurtures contemplation in a context that is in important respects spiritually and practically egalitarian. And so the awkward and embarrassing 'otherness' of the female contemplative, challenging conventions and boundaries, comes to be a sign of the deeper and unsettling otherness of the contemplative life as such, its refusal to be instrumentalised in the service of a divided social order. Teresa's typology intriguingly brings together the scandal of 'Magdalene' as a displaced gentlewoman, abandoning her family and the walls of her household to go in search of Jesus, with the scandal of her listening to Jesus in contemplative silence. As we have noted, *Castle* 7.4.13 evokes this vividly: 'Do you think it would be a small mortification for a woman of nobility like her to wander through these streets (and perhaps alone because her fervent love had made her unaware of what she was doing) and enter a house she had never entered before and afterward suffer the criticism of the Pharisee and the very many other things she must have suffered? ... If nowadays there is so much gossip against persons who are not so notorious, what would have been said then?' Her humiliation as a transgressive woman is part of her preparation for contemplative silence, a suffering that detaches the soul from obsession with its solidity and status.

Notice that Teresa suggests that Mary's intense love makes her unaware of what she is doing; it is not a casual point. If a woman causes scandal by adopting a religious life on Teresa's model, this is because she is overwhelmed by the divine imperative. As elsewhere, Teresa wants to stress that her actions are not a deliberate campaign against ecclesiastical discipline, but primarily a response to the initiative of Christ. And the imagery of 'wandering through the streets' – imagery intriguingly paralleled in the use of the Song of Songs (3.2: 'I will get up now and go about the city, through its streets and squares; I will search for the one my heart loves') in the liturgy for St Mary Magdalene's feast – tacitly recognises the gravity of the reproach: Magdalene may be a repentant prostitute, but in this respect at least she continues in her old habits.[5] Only Christ's welcoming gestures and words will establish her identity as a transformed sinner; her behaviour appears ambiguous. Teresa is being bold here, anticipating the most destructive criticism possible and turning its flank. For her sisters, clarity about the reputational risk of this life is essential and she deliberately underlines it: if the search for God in the reformed Carmel will be compared by critics to the humiliation of prostitution, this is all part of the preparation for that ultimate displacement of the self and its images that occurs in interior prayer.

Teresa's biblical models allow her here to make some very strong points about contemplation, not only for women but for all believers. From the point of view of ordinary social exchange and the mutual securing of status and power, contemplation will sooner or later appear as a dangerous and suspect affair. And when the socially constrained figure of a woman (especially a woman of putatively 'good' family) is involved, the otherness and unsettling character of contemplation is particularly marked. For men, the issues of exposure and scandal are not the same; and Teresa's response to John of the Cross about access to Jesus has so strong a gendered character that it is as if she is saying that there is something about the contemplative calling which only women – and particularly women who are or have made themselves marginal to their inherited systems or structures – can demonstrate; not because of some 'essentialist' notion of the female as more naturally contemplative (not an idea that would have made sense in Teresa's day), but because of the issues of status and danger that arise where the female contemplative is concerned. She is not constructing a general theology of the standing of the contemplative in the Church, but she is unmistakeably constructing a foundation for such a theology, if only by the close linkage she makes between the contemplative community's repudiation of 'honour' as a social marker and the possibility of growth towards union. For the further stages of the *Castle*'s journey to happen, what is needed is a dissolution of secure and enclosed images of identity over against God; the rupture with a society obsessed with managing and negotiating such images is a beginning for this deeper rupture.[6] And the scheme leads us to recognise that the contemplative as such is always 'other', not in the

sense of superiority on a single scale but as representing the novelty of the society that Christ creates, the
'college' of the apostles.

As a reader of the Gospels, then, Teresa is in search
of material that will provide a theological account of
this novelty, and also a narrative and imaginative rationale for the disruption that response to a contemplative
calling entails – most dramatically through the figures
to which she returns so many times, the problematic
and challenging female figures who approach Jesus and
are welcomed. Part of her theological legacy is here in
this subtle use of such figures to suggest an ecclesiology
as well as a theology of the contemplative calling. The
Catholic Church is primitively a community in which
kinship with Christ is the supreme defining category,
so that any other natural distinction of race, family or
indeed gender is put in question. And the contemplative
life is at the heart of the unremitting task of reminding the
Church to be what it is in relation to Christ's invitation,
because it is a life that requires the most fundamental loss of self-based solidity or security, a faithful and
sacrificial response to divine fidelity. As I hope to show
elsewhere at greater length, this can be connected with
the foundations of a Teresian theology of the Eucharist
as the sacrament of divine fidelity within the Church and
the soul, the tangible promise of God's refusal to abandon world, self or Church. But in our present context of
thinking about Teresa and the Gospels, it is clear that
contemplative life in poverty, outside the familiar forms
of the patronage system, is being highlighted as one of
those things that most clearly reminds the Church of its
very identity as the 'kindred' of Jesus. The contemplative calling in the Church, making the Church other to

its habitual, routinised self, recalls the basic otherness of the Church to fallen creation (especially status-ridden society); and its living-out by women under the Teresian discipline makes this particularly clear. If the sixteenth-century Spanish Church wanted to deny women the contemplative life in its full Teresian radicality, something essential for both Gospel and Church is lost in Teresa's eyes; the unsettling universalism of the 'college of Christ' is to a significant extent absorbed back into the habits of a rivalrous and anxious society.

And if that radical vision does not inform the understanding of the contemplative calling wherever it is responded to, contemplation will be in danger of becoming a search for just the wrong sort of 'interiority' and just the wrong sort of achievement – a private spiritual journey with only a tangential relation to the integrity of the Church as a whole, and, at worst, a programme of individual spiritual refinement which could create new kinds of hierarchy and new kinds of division. Teresa clearly finds it impossible to separate out her theology of contemplation from her ecclesiology – even though she would probably not have wanted to frame her own thought in such terms. The priority of Christ's invitation is what creates both the new community of grace and the new de-centred subject that emerges in the long process of contemplative maturation. It would be worse than eccentric to separate them, and a proper 'evangelical' understanding of both is needed (now as then) to prevent the theology of interior prayer from becoming indulgent or sentimental and the theology of transfigured community from becoming activist and self-reliant.

11

TERESA AND THE EUCHARIST

Teresa of Avila is indisputably a figure whose influence and attraction have been extensive beyond the limits of the Roman Catholic Church. In addition to the (admittedly not very adequate) discussion of her by William James in his *Varieties of Religious Experience*, and Vita Sackville-West's idiosyncratic but sympathetic study in *The Eagle and the Dove*, we have the enormous labours of Edgar Allison Peers, an Anglican, as editor and translator of her letters and author of a luminous brief study of her life;[1] and also a magisterial essay by another Anglican, E. W. Trueman Dicken, still one of the fullest comparisons in English of the schemes of spiritual ascent in Teresa and John of the Cross.[2] Yet this ecumenical appeal has its ironic side. Teresa herself, as her comments (especially in *The Way of Perfection*) amply demonstrate, saw the Reformation as an unequivocal disaster. What she was primarily aware of was the spiralling violence between Catholic and Reformed just north of the Pyrenees; and for her the Reformation was more or less coterminous with a 'Lutheran' revolt not only against ecclesiastical authority but – far more importantly – against sacramental religion, a matter of the destruction of churches and the discarding of the reserved sacrament. She tells us at the start of the *Way* (1.2)[3] that she learned of the religious violence in France as she began her reforming work, and that it spurred her to intensify the austerity and poverty of the new communities as an act of reparation for the 'Lutheran' rebellion and all that it brought with it.[4] A little further on (3.8), she elaborates this, in the context of a treatment of how Christ is to be honoured: 'Human forces', she writes, 'are not sufficient to stop the spread of this fire caused by these heretics' (3.1);[5] and so the sisters must pray that the life of contemplation in the Teresian Carmel will strengthen the hand of those who resist more publicly the dissolution of true religion. God must be petitioned to safeguard his honour, or, more specifically, the honour of his Son, who has already endured so many dishonours and humiliations for our sake (3.7). The faithfulness of the sisters to their rule is a witness to the honour of God, and by keeping them faithful, God secures his honour. And this is a matter of some urgency: the destruction of churches elsewhere in Europe means that Christ is threatened with homelessness, just as on earth he had no place to lay his head (3.8): how can the Father tolerate this? Has Christ not already suffered all he needs to? What is happening is that human beings are losing those places Christ has 'for inviting his friends'[6] – churches imagined as places of refuge where the weak or displaced may find food. Is all this a punishment for our continuing sin? If so, we must pray and offer our own poverty to God so that he will act to 'defend' his Son.

Thus the project of the Teresian Carmel is defined as a response to what Teresa sees as the crisis of Eucharistic faith and devotion provoked by the Reformers: Christ is being dishonoured and cast out; the Teresian community must therefore honour and welcome him all the more, not only to make reparation for these injuries but to 'persuade' God to defend his honour – that is (since Teresa is not simple-minded about prayer), to allow God space to act more fully and visibly in the world by withdrawing from our own selfish preoccupations and coming to him in emptiness of spirit. As we shall see, this means ultimately that the community itself becomes a kind of Eucharistic demonstration, a place of invitation such as the Church itself is meant to be. If Christ is made homeless anew by the violence of the Reformers, he will have a home in the community where his invitation is heard and honoured, and where the Eucharistic promise of Christ's faithful presence in our midst is made plain once more. The heart of Teresa's treatment of this is to be found in chapters 33 to 35 of the *Way*, where she meditates on the petition in the Lord's Prayer for daily bread. This section of the text begins and ends with the same allusions to 'Lutheran' violence as we find at the beginning of the book. We pray for the daily renewal of Christ's presence in the Eucharist; but this is a prayer for the daily renewal of his vulnerability and humiliation. 'How many insults will be committed today against this Most Blessed Sacrament! In how many enemies' hands must the Father see Him! How much irreverence from these heretics!'(33.3).[7] 'He allows Himself to be crushed to pieces each day' (33.4).[8] And if he is silent on his own behalf and speaks only for us, it is surely for us to speak for him;[9] yet this is *Christ's* prayer, and it is thus a prayer that he will not be taken from us and from the world in which he has elected to remain: 'He asks the Father not to take Him from us until the end of the world'.[10] And at the end of the section (3.3–4), Teresa repeats, with even more fervour, her prayer that God will halt the rising tide of blasphemy and be mindful of what it means that his Son is still in the world. As we have seen, we cannot pray that the Son be removed from the world; so, unless God brings the world to an end, he must surely bring the humiliations of his Son an end (35.4). But it is our task to make that possible for him, so to speak, by our openness to his action; and by this point in the argument, that openness is not any longer primarily through the austerity of the monastic discipline but through pleading the gift and sacrifice that Christ himself is making in the Eucharist. Teresa has begun by stressing the idea of the community's discipline as reparation; but it is clear by the end of the discussion that what is effective with God is not any human agency but the prayer of Christ himself in the Eucharist. The sisters are not simply to be exemplary ascetics; the crucial point is that they be *exemplary receivers of the Eucharist*. They should 'not be seen in this world without Him' (34.2);[11] they are now his 'house' (34.7–8), the vehicle of Christ's presence, so that we may expect miracles to occur, especially answers to prayer.[12] Rather ironically, her insistent passion for a 'Eucharistic' response to the crisis of the Reformation has produced a theology of the Eucharist that is in some ways highly congruent with the Reformed emphasis on the exclusively divine nature of the action that takes place at the altar: human effort and self-denial give way to the prayer of God to God in the sacramental event.

But what of course marks out this theology as, ultimately, different from the Protestant consensus is the continuing stress on the abiding presence of Christ in the elements. As Teresa elaborates her Eucharistic vision in these chapters of the *Way*, she sketches a theology in which the unbroken sacramental presence acts as a token of the eternal mission of God the Son. As she puts it in 33.5, the incarnate Christ 'reminds' the Father that he eternally belongs to the Father as the vehicle of the Father's will; the Father therefore is wholly free to go on sending the Son into the world to accomplish the salvation the Father desires. Christ in the Eucharist prays to go on being 'sent' – which is to go on being what he eternally is, the one who is sent by the Father; he prays to go on being his eternal self, we might say. But he prays to go on being his *incarnate* self also, to continue in the form of a slave: 'there is no slave who would willingly say he is a slave, and yet it seems that Jesus is honoured to be one'.[13] In Jesus's name we ask to be given our *daily* bread. But in the light of these theological considerations, we must recognise that the 'day' in question 'lasts as long as the world and no longer' (34.2).[14] Christ petitions the Father to be allowed to spend the entire day of creation's history 'in servitude' or 'slavery', the slavery of being wholly at our disposal through 'the manna and nourishment of His humanity'.[15] Thus we can say that Teresa's Eucharistic theology is strikingly Chalcedonian: the Eucharist makes sense because of Christ's dual nature. He is, in the first place, the one who is eternally the faithful respondent to the Father's will, who is, in Augustinian terms, the one who eternally knows that he is 'from' the Father[16] and so is able to perform in his life on earth what the Father intends, since there is nothing he knows of himself that is not to do with the Father's will. And he is simultaneously the one who is in complete solidarity with humanity – a solidarity shown in his patient enduring of the wounds and insults that are given him in his incarnate identity as also now in his ignored and abused sacramental identity. Understanding the Eucharist in Teresa's terms requires us, it seems, to grasp both the eternal ground of Christ's obedience in his being wholly at the Father's disposal, and the specific shape this takes in the unshakeable decision to be with us for as long as creation endures.

Teresa's emphasis on the present actuality of Christ in the sacrament leads her to reject the idea that there would be any profit in being a literal contemporary of Jesus in the days of his flesh (34.6): Jesus is no less present in the sacrament than in Galilee. It is – another irony – rather reminiscent of the Lutheran Kierkegaard's argument in the *Philosophical Fragments*[17] that there is no spiritual advantage to being contemporary with the event of revelation because of the absolute hiddenness of the divine presence in its incarnate form. Teresa goes on to reflect on the fallacy of valuing more deeply some image of Christ than the presence of Christ in the sacrament: our imagination may provide us with pictures of what happened in the earthly life of Jesus ('We picture within ourselves how things happened to Him in the past'),[18] but receiving communion is an event that is happening *now*. The Eucharistic presence is not, of course, visually or tangibly 'like' what we imagine about Christ's life or indeed about his heavenly state. But, Teresa argues, given that we literally cannot now see him as he was in Galilee, and since the only alternative is seeing him in his present glory, it should be clear that sacramental presence is all that is possible: we are not capable of bearing the sight of his glory while we live in this world. So Christ makes himself 'easy to deal with', in Teresa's bold phrase (34.9).[19] In his 'disguise' of the consecrated elements, he can be approached without fear or embarrassment or excessive formality, like a monarch going among his people. And when we have received communion, that is the time when we can most readily come to him in prayer: at such a time, praying to an image of Christ makes no sense (34.11): 'You would be leaving the Person Himself in order to look at a picture of Him.'[20] We don't turn our eyes from a loved person when they are with us in order to look at pictures of them, and images of Christ are helpful precisely when we have no sense or assurance of his presence (Teresa notes in passing that this is another problem with Reformation iconoclasm). But after communion, we turn our eyes inwards: he will show himself to the soul, even if not in the obvious visual sense (34.10).

In the next chapter, Teresa elaborates further on this. It is possible that this post-communion period will not be as satisfyingly 'devotional' as some other exercises (35.2); but it is essential to remain with the presence that has been given. Not the least important reason for this is that in so doing we reflect back to Christ the selfless fidelity that he has shown to us in the Eucharistic gift. He has stayed with us; it is now for us to stay with him, as a form of suffering for and with him. Our accompanying of him is a witness to his faithfulness at a time when many violently reject him or walk away from him. The language of this section of the chapter is reminiscent of John of the Cross in the famous exhortation in Book II.7 of *The Ascent of Mount Carmel*: we cannot expect that the discipleship of the crucified Christ will be without cost to us; we cannot pray to be spared what Christ was not spared. But what is distinctive is that

Teresa locates this thought so firmly in the context of her Eucharistic meditations: the sacramental presence is for her the immediate actuality of Christ's suffering for us; it is as direct an embodiment of his solidarity and vulnerability as the incarnation itself, a reminder to us that the costly divine will to be with us extends to the end of the world. We are returned to her earlier theme of Christ's 'honour': who except us will speak for him to the Father, praying for an end to his humiliation (35.3)? And we do so, not on the grounds of our own merit or fervency, but because of the gift already given, the presence both incarnate and sacramental of the one who is sent by the Father in eternity and history alike.

As this summary shows, Teresa's doctrine of the Eucharist is complex and coherent. It rests upon a clear traditional Christology, in which both the divinity and the humanity of Christ are essential for our understanding. Christ is primordially the personal form of the Father's will; in a sense, he *is* the divine 'mission', wholly expressing and communicating the divine life as it moves outwards into creation. But he is equally the embodied form of divine solidarity with the human condition: the Eucharistic presence is the way in which this solidarity is to be realised even when the specific incarnate reality is no longer there to be seen or sensed. And what secures the continuity of incarnation and sacrament is the 'form of a slave' which they share: Christ's incarnate humanity exists simply to be for us; likewise his sacramental presence is at our service and for our nourishment. Some later writers have used the silence, the materiality, the extreme physical fragility of the sacramental elements to cast light on what the *forma servi* means in the incarnation itself, and this is very much in the spirit of Teresa's reflections. And, as she notes in VI.7 of the *Interior Castle*, any piety that seeks to relativise or diminish the significance of Christ's humanity because of a false and misconceived valuation of spirit over body, will end in a loss of devotion to the sacrament. In simple terms, if it matters that Christ took flesh, it matters that he continues to be in some sense materially present; if the taking of flesh is simply instrumental to a purely 'spiritual' goal, the sacraments are of no importance. Thus the Eucharist affirms the necessity of not turning away from the life of the body, as this is where Christ's fidelity to creation is continuously affirmed and enacted. At the same time, the Eucharist affirms and enacts the presence of Christ in the soul. When we have received the sacrament, we know that Christ inhabits the soul in ways that our senses will not grasp; at that moment, the underlying presence of God in us is activated in a new way by the gift of Christ's coming.

Teresa returns to the subject in *Interior Castle* V.1, where she contrasts the Eucharistic encounter with what happens in certain stages of contemplation. The gifts that are given to the soul in the fifth mansions include brief passages in which the ordinary operations of soul (and to some extent body) are slowed or suspended and a diffuse but overwhelmingly powerful awareness of God's presence arises. Teresa struggles to make it clear that this is an awareness of God's abiding inhabitation of the soul by 'presence, power, and essence' (V.1.10), not a presence by grace, in the sense of a passing visitation: what is happening is that the soul becomes aware of what is abidingly true at its centre. She distinguishes it (V.1.11) from the 'certitude' that we feel about the bodily presence of Christ in the sacrament: we do not, in contemplation, apprehend any material vehicle of God's pervasive presence – nor could we, if we think through what a *pervasive* presence must mean. The fifth mansion sense of union with God is very carefully characterised as not being connected with only one faculty or subdivision of the self. It could be said that it is what some call a 'non-dual' awareness: a self-consciousness in which consciousness of God is inseparable from the bare fact of consciousness itself. But, connecting this with what has been said in the *Way*, we can conclude, not that the Eucharistic event is in some way more 'limited' or earthbound than the fifth mansion level of union, but that the gift of Christ's sacramental action is a gift in which – whatever stage of contemplative maturity we have reached – the abiding presence of God in the self is brought alive in a fresh way. In other words, *the sacrament does not bring Christ to a place where God is absent*. And clarity about God's omnipresence is not something that *replaces* a localised view of presence or action as in the sacrament or the incarnation: what Teresa is doing is, in effect, denying a model of grace which sees no farther than occasional divine incursions into a neutral finite territory that needs to be colonised.

This helps to make sense of an intriguing text from (probably) 1575,[21] in which Teresa speaks of the Father 'receiving' Christ in our soul when we take communion. This is an unusual, perhaps unique, idea: Teresa asserts that Christ's divinity is already in the soul – as her discussion in the *Castle* would lead us to believe – but that his humanity is not. Thus within the soul the entire Trinity is always present; what is new and distinctive about the gift of Christ in the sacrament is that the self-giving accomplished in his earthly life and death is here re-presented. He comes to the Father in the soul just as he comes to the Father's throne in heaven, bringing his incarnate humanity with him.[22] What happens in the Mass is the incorporation of human history into divine life, as the historical enacting in Jesus of the Son's gift to the Father is recapitulated. The abiding presence of the Trinity in the soul is awakened by the Son's 'passing through' the texture of historical existence, not only in the once and for all event of incarnation and passion but also in the actual humanity of the communicant. Teresa does not attempt to work out exactly how the sacramental gift correlates with the intensified awareness of the continuing divine presence in the fifth mansions, but it would make sense to see the Eucharistic encounter as the necessary normal condition for the contemplative gift: the reconciling work of Christ is realised afresh in the Mass, so that the created soul may become a sharer in the life of the Trinity not only as participating in the general presence of God in creatures as their ground and sustainer but also as participating in the actual interrelation of the divine persons. The awareness of intensified union with God as described in the fifth mansions is the bliss or ecstasy that the Father purposes for his human creatures; and the possibility of this is precisely what is restored in the incarnate Christ and so in the Eucharist. Teresa's idiom in this brief passage may be unusual, but the underlying theology is of a piece with all she has said in the *Way*.

The final point to be noted in her Eucharistic synthesis is her stress on endurance in what may be unpromising or unrewarding internal conditions. The Eucharist embodies Christ's vulnerability to the human world and its vicissitudes; our readiness to abide with his sacramental presence and not to look for easier and consolatory forms of spiritual exercise after communion is another distinctive Teresian emphasis. Fidelity to the incarnate Christ – a theme she has already flagged in the *Life* in a rather different context[23] – is manifested in this willingness to mirror Christ's decision to stay with us in spite of humiliation and pain and loss of honour. It is both the effect and sign of his prior fidelity; and as such it represents our sharing by grace in his transfigured humanity and its offering to the Father. We become acceptable advocates because we are more fully in him as receivers of his sacramental life. Thus our suffering has no independent force with God, and we should not strictly speak about 'reparation' as though this were something we could achieve. The tightly woven paradox is that we can only plead with God to spare Christ his humiliation by becoming more deeply grounded in what that humiliation makes possible for us: his vulnerability to the violence of the Reformers is exactly what gives us the capacity to plead effectively for an end to the fire, storm and turmoil of the age. 'What is there for me to do, my Creator, but offer this most blessed bread to You, and even though You have given it to us, return it to You and beg You through the merits of Your Son to grant me this favour.'[24]

Teresa knew little, if anything, about the actual theology of the Reformers – as is evident from her indiscriminate use of 'Lutherans' to describe the very un-Lutheran Protestants of France as well as the more distant and exotic heretics of Northern Europe. And in one sense her concern is not at all with Reformed theology; it is with an 'ideal type', a myth, we might say, a way of imagining a style of ostensibly Christian piety that is in fact stripped of its Christian essentials. This ideal heresy is a rejection of the idea of the Church as a home into which Christ invites the hungry; and for Teresa it is obvious that if the Church is to be such a home it must be literally a house in which the sacrament is both celebrated and reserved for adoration. As we have seen, she cannot easily be charged with a reduction of the sacrament to an object 'confected' by priestly agency; her emphasis is consistently on the will and action of God in the sacrament, on the Eucharistic bread as a dynamic sign of a promise that is actively being kept. The heart of her Eucharistic thought is that our prayer is effective because and only because of Christ's decision to be perpetually with us, and that the unbroken continuity of Eucharistic practice in the Church as well as the continuity of the material presence of the consecrated elements bear witness to this in the simplest and most concrete way imaginable. Her defence of the traditional Catholic approach is predicated on a strong doctrine of the priority and sovereignty of grace that rests on as little 'synergy' between divine and human as any Protestant could want.

What sets this most decisively apart from the classical Reformed perspective on the Eucharist is, of course, the uncompromising stress on the materiality of Christ's presence (and the consequent stress on veneration for the reserved sacrament). But this being said, it is not impossible to see Teresa's theology in this area as a ground for ecumenical rapprochement: she makes it plain that we cannot assume that any theology of substantial divine presence in the sacrament must be superstitious or 'materialistic' in the way that sixteenth century Reformed polemic assumes. Teresa unmistakeably identifies the effective action of the Eucharistic sacrifice as that of Christ alone; but she does also see the physicality of the Eucharistic presence as the contemporary form of Christ's incarnate vulnerability, his direct involvement with the active evil will of fallen humanity – where Calvin (say) would have insisted on a 'real absence' in the Eucharist of that specific form of vulnerability and pointed us to the agency, in that context, of the risen and glorified Christ. The question then becomes one of how Christ's suffering, Christ's *forma servi*, is to be understood in relation to his sovereign action and initiative in the Eucharist as elsewhere. Teresa, it might be said, is implicitly proposing that continuing vulnerability is precisely the shape of the Son's freedom in action – in the sacrament as in the act of incarnation itself.

These are technicalities which Teresa would not have been interested in as such; but they suggest ways in which her distinctive Eucharistic themes provide material for a deeper ecumenical conversation. As so often in her writings, Teresa constructs her significant theological insights through what we could call a 'staged' dialogue with God – protest, plea, a doubling-back to question the ground of the protest, a renewed and changed petition. God cannot intend the continued suffering and dishonour of his Son; let the Son be spared! But the Son's continuing presence in the face of humiliation is our assurance of his unbreakable decision to be with us, and if he is not with us, we can make no effective prayer. The Eucharist becomes both a sign of his continuing self-emptying and the divine act that enables us to pray effectively that his honour will be saved; and it will be saved by our honouring and housing him when he is humiliated now as he was in his earthly passion.

This staged meditation is designed to lead us into a fuller and more grounded recognition of our incapacity to make a difference on our own – even to make reparation to God for his damaged honour; and so it leads into a deeper apprehension of the priority of divine act in all our praying, just as in the Eucharist we give God what is already his gift to us (a familiar liturgical theme). Faced with a classical Protestant objection to what sounds like synergy between divine and human action, or with the rhetoric of making a human offering (of meritorious asceticism, for example) to God that will be efficacious in some way, Teresa would have agreed with the concern; but she would, on the evidence of her writing, have maintained that the actual recognition of divine sovereignty and priority can only be reached through the trial and self-correction of the drama she outlines. Human outrage or sympathy or anxiety have to be enunciated first, before they can be dissolved in the acknowledgment of all-sufficient divine agency; like Teresa herself, we must first be moved by the sense of Christ's isolation and need; we must respond with generosity and with the willingness to stand as witnesses alongside the suffering Christ (and so not respond with violence directed against the enemies of Christ); and then we must recognize that our very freedom to stand in witness and plead with the Father is his act, crystallised in his faithful Eucharistic 'abiding'. This is not a Reformed theology; but it is very distant from the caricature of 'Pelagian' confidence in the capacity of finite agents to change the mind of God which the Reformers so objected to.

Teresa saw the Eucharistic faithfulness of her sisters – communicating, meditating on the Christ received in communion, adoring the Christ continuously present in the reserved sacrament – as the best response possible to what she believed to be a revolt against the very foundation of the visible Church and ultimately against the Incarnation itself. Christ is being deprived of the houses where he welcomes the spiritually hungry and needy, and so the Teresian communities must be Eucharistic 'homes' for him, witnessing to his unchanging invitation and gift; and their prayer must be, not that the Father protect Christ from humiliation and vindicate his honour (as she originally affirms in her protest to God), but that we shall be faithful in our contemplative appropriation of the gift received in the Eucharist, which is the realisation in us of the active relation between Father and Son in the Trinity, and so become more transparent to the divine act of saving self-emptying, for the sake of the world. Whatever the polemical edge of her thoughts on all this, it is possible, so I have argued, to take her sophisticated analysis of the meaning of the daily bread of the sacrament and use it to sharpen and deepen an ecumenical conversation about grace and freedom and human capacity, uniting sacramental theology with what is done in and for us in the unfolding gifts of contemplative intimacy, the exploration of which is Teresa's most evident and precious legacy to Christians of all confessions.

PART FIVE

WAYS OF KNOWING

12

Julian of Norwich's Way

Julian's immense appeal to most readers is that she represents in some sense a theology that leads into contemplative awareness; uninterested in winning arguments and consolidating formulae, she speaks repeatedly of what she *sees* and what is 'shown'. The mind or sensibility she embodies is a receptive one, taking time to absorb what has been manifested. One point that's perhaps worth noting specially in this context is to do with the very word 'Revelation' as the title of the Longer Version: we might well take it for granted that a 'revelation' was what settled questions, an ending of uncertainty; but this text is the record of a lengthy and patient investigating of the initial vision. To encounter revelation, it seems, is to be launched on a process of interwoven divine gift and human exploration – which casts a fresh light on what we might want to say about the fundamental Christian revelation itself. To claim that we receive revelation is not – on this basis – to assert that we are in possession of answers not provided to others, but to say that we have been impelled by the act of God into this unfolding process of reflection and growth. And what we know 'by' or 'through' revelation becomes inseparable from the time it takes to reflect and grow.

But this prompts me to suggest that one useful way of reading Julian of Norwich is to think of her as writing an 'anti-theology'. Let me be clear: I'm definitely not disagreeing with those – most recently and superbly Denys Turner[1] – who have teased out the basic theological themes in Julian and demonstrated their coherence and intellectual power, as well as their rootedness in classical Christian categories. I am not suggesting that Julian is indifferent to doctrine, a writer who is interesting because of her rhetoric not her substance, an enemy to systematic thinking or, worst of all, a 'poetic' writer who need not be held accountable for her consistency. Julian is not, thank goodness, a devotional author; she is manifestly thinking hard and expects her readers to think hard. But it is a very particular kind of thinking. She is (and here I follow the definitive work of Vincent Gillespie and Maggie Ross above all)[2] inviting her readers to ask themselves whether they are asking the right questions; offering an 'anti-theology' in the sense that she is repeatedly turning upside-down the structure that *unthinking* theology takes for granted and challenging us to recognise that the perceptions and feelings induced by this unthinking theology are dismantled by letting yourself be *shown* the truth that all theology gestures towards. In one obvious way, her writing reverses expectation by presenting itself as a kind of seminar conducted by the voice of Jesus: the difficult and 'dismantling' insights which are offered by that voice make for a protracted exploration, in the course of which certain problems disappear. They are not problems to *solve,* simply because what makes them problems in the first place is a distorted sense of what theology is and a clouded awareness of the fundamental events and insights of Christian identity. A great deal of habitual theological noise therefore has to be silenced if truth is really to be shown.

One or two examples out of many: in chapter xxii, Jesus asks Julian if she is 'well apaid' that he has suffered for her; and when she responds positively, he says, 'If thou art apaide, I am apaide.'[3] Theology has typically agonised over what it would take to satisfy God, to 'pay the price of sin'; and the unthinking use of such a theological notion may leave us with the familiar anxiety that God is faced with squaring a circle in which God has to 'do justice' to his own justice, his own mercy and our guilt. God must – so to speak – pay himself a fair price. The theological conundrum is how to do so and yet enact his merciful will. Julian's anti-theological perspective is to turn this entirely on its head and present the situation as though the anxiety and the circle-squaring challenge lay not with God but with us: can *we* be satisfied? Because if we are, God is. And, as she goes on to think through the 'thre hevens' that she is shown, the three dimensions of divine bliss, she almost casually offers us another upside-down perspective in saying that we are not only Christ's bliss but also his 'mede': we are what the Father gives him as the 'reward' of his selfless love as shown in the cross. Instead of a scheme in which divine justice is satisfied and eternal life for us is secured by the atonement performed on the cross, it is more that human need is satisfied, and joy for the glorified Christ is secured by the Father giving him the redeemed human family as a 'crowne' (a particularly powerful image, as Nicholas Watson notes in his edition,[4] given the crucial importance at the very beginning of the visions of the sight of the crown of thorns and its savage wounds).

The theme of redeemed humanity as Christ's joy and crown recurs (in, for example, chapter xxxi, where the final reconciliation of all is the assuaging of Christ's 'love-longing' and 'thurste'). Julian is recasting the theological pattern so that what needs to be 'satisfied' can be seen simultaneously in double perspective, in a binocular way: what must be satisfied is on the one hand the divine yearning for us, created to reflect the divine joy to itself; on the other it is our own poverty as fallen creatures that calls down divine action to fill its void. If we acknowledge the divine act that presses on us to fill our emptiness, we are in the process of becoming the reflection of divine joy. We are 'satisfying' God's longing, just as our own hunger is satisfied: 'If thou art apaide, I am apaide.' This echoes, unconsciously, the familiar Irenaean maxim that 'the glory of God is the human being fully alive',[5] but gives it a new and subtle twist. Most importantly of all, without simply ignoring the received language for understanding the process of redemption, it reworks the story so that it is no longer a matter of a conundrum to be solved, incompatible requirements to be met. The business of satisfaction is radically simple – though far from simple for us to absorb or even believe. It is not that God is faced with a challenge to which the ingenious stratagem of a suffering that has infinite merit is the answer, in Anselmian mode; the challenge is posed to us. Are we content to believe that we are loved? Because if not, there is always more love to meet our need: if there were more to do and suffer, 'love shulde never let him have rest tille he had done it' (xxii), and however much had so far been done and suffered would still seem like nothing in comparison, because there is infinite resource to pour into the human void.

To call this, as I have done, 'anti-theology' doesn't mean that Julian is deliberately developing an alternative to Anselm's theology of atonement or even Aquinas's; she is mostly innocent of controversy over such matters. Her point is to spring us from the trap of imagining a God faced with some kind of conceptual impasse, and to force us to ask whether the conundrum we seek to solve theologically isn't in fact the result of our failing to grasp that the entire logic of salvation depends on the basic fact of unconditional and unconstrained love – the sheer desire of God for divine love to be shared with what he has made and the sheer liberty to enter into the self-made void of human misery in order to change the human landscape. Satisfaction has become less to do with honouring eternal demands, more like the 'atonement' memorably described by Geoffrey Hill in a famous lecture on poetry:[6] 'selfhood being made at one with itself' in the very act of writing, a definition given deep theological resonance by the way in which T. S. Eliot, in a passage quoted by Hill,[7] can describe this as an act of 'appeasement, of absolution, and of something very like near annihilation'. 'Appeasement': something is pacified or stilled in the words uttered, something restless and struggling in our language is settled. To be 'apaide' in Julian's theological world is to discover that we cannot pull apart human need and divine self-enactment and make them struggle for resolution: for God to be, actively, God is eternally for God to act for the articulating and embodying of his 'bliss', his 'heven', and so to be always already active for the absolving of our self-generated disasters (c.f. chapter liii, 'God began never to love mankind'). God's selfhood *is* unchangingly itself in this action, and our selfhood becomes itself in

173

our recognition of what it is for God to be God. As in the poem, for Hill and Eliot, so in the act and words of faith: appeasement occurs and something is 'annihilated'. More about this later.

But these thoughts take us directly to a cluster of ideas and images around divine action in the *Revelation*. The well-known passage where Julian denies that there is anger in God (xlix) immediately poses the question, 'So where *is* anger?' Julian is clear that if God were to feel anger for even a moment, he would cease to be creator; we should not exist. Anger happens in us; it is that atmosphere of bitter conflict and fear which holds us away from peace, being at one with ourselves, living in atonement. If God were part of the constantly renewed climate of conflict and fear ('wrath and the contrariousness that is in us') in which we live, if God's vision of us were like our vision of others *and of him*, how could we make sense of our dependence for our very being on eternal unanxious generosity? Once again, what Julian is doing is to steer us towards what alone will make sense of the fundamental shape of the Christian narrative: in chapters xlvii and xlviii, she has set out the puzzle: what does it mean for God to turn away from his anger towards forgiveness? The more we are aware of how we are sustained in being by unconditional generous love (the Holy Spirit as 'endless life wonning in oure soule', xlviii), the less we can imagine anger as a state of divine life. Thus it must be our own resistance to life or grace, our 'contrariousness to pees and to love' (ibid.); just as in the discussion of 'satisfaction', the problem turns out to be in us, not in God or in some abstract realm in which offences are weighed and calculated. Once again, Julian offers us an anti-theology. Stop thinking about how God can solve the problem and focus instead on the problem that is your own 'contrariousness', your own unwillingness to be 'apaide'.

Our redemption is, we have seen, not a skilful stratagem devised to keep the metaphysical or moral lawyers happy, but the sheer outworking of who or what God is. Hence, in the great 'Lord and servant' meditation of chapter li, the extraordinary fusion (binocular vision again) of the fall of Adam and the Incarnation itself: 'When Adam fell, Godes sonne fell.' Because human identity is eternally decreed to be the inseparable companion of Christ's joy (we could compare this with the way the same theme is developed in St John of the Cross's *Romanzas*),[8] the disaster that overtakes Adam is simultaneously the journey of the Son of God to earth and hell; what happens to Adam happens to the Second Person of the Trinity. So – to pick up again the theme we looked at a little while back – we find we cannot pull apart the human condition and the action of God. We cannot think of the latter as an afterthought or even in the strict sense a 'response' to the former. 'God began never to love mankind'; for us to be loved is simply for us *to be what we are* in the face of a God *who is what he is*. Hence Julian's rather startling statement in xlix that God 'as aneynt himself may not forgeve': as far as God's own 'Godness' is concerned, the categories of offence and forgiveness as we usually apply them are not appropriate. There is no resentment to overcome, no process by which God becomes able to put anger behind him, and so on.

And this connects with one of Julian's most pervasive themes, the theme which Denys Turner rightly sees as fundamental to her theodicy.[9] 'Our lord God doth all' (xi): and if all that is done or enacted is God's doing, sin cannot be an act ('sinne is no dede'). God is the mid-point of all, and so whatever exists participates in his act insofar as it is itself active. Hence Julian's emphasis that our nature is complete or perfect 'in God': 'oure kinde is in God hole' (lvii), and indeed is in a sense indistinguishable from God. 'I saw no difference between God and oure substance, but as it were all God' (liv). As Turner has shown so well, this is not a sudden swerve into pantheism, simply the recognition of a basic point of Christian metaphysics.[10] If our active existence as creatures is dependent on the uncreated act of God, we cannot expect to see divine action and created action as if they were two things side by side, distinguishable by having different characteristics (being infinite isn't a *characteristic*, nor is being created). And this is the deep philosophical rationale for the inseparability between Adam's fall and the Incarnation of God the Son: that outpouring of divine act which makes the world overall, and the crown of created existence that is rational humanity, is strictly the same act by which the Son is what and who he is; for the Son to be the Son is for the Son to be the one who has always been the lover and companion of Adam's race. Pull this apart and once again you have a set of puzzles to be solved. Julian's anti-theology relentlessly insists that you think again about the theological questions that seem most obvious and pressing; and this also means insisting that you look at yourself as questioner and try to see more clearly why you so obsessively frame your anxieties in this way. The apparent theological Gordian knots we confront yield, not to strenuous conceptual refinement, but to radical re-casting of the questions – which is also a matter of the radical re-casting of who we think we are and what we think we do.

Julian's thought is dangerously easy to represent simply as the gentle and affirming revision of a harsh orthodoxy; but the energy of such an anti-theology is in fact a troubling and unsettling affair. It directs our attention to our own refusal to believe that what we most basically are is the objects of love; to avoid facing this, we commit ourselves to an anger, a 'contrariousness' or spirit of contradiction, that allows us to keep the love of God at arm's length and to imagine a God whose requirements paint him into a corner. We tell what is admittedly quite a compelling story about how God, so to speak, makes himself able to accept us – how God becomes at one with himself. In other words, we project on to God the story that is in fact ours; we project the difficulty of atonement on to a supposed divine agent who needs to rearrange the world in order to be what he ought to be, or to be in the relationship he ought to be in with the created universe. If the obstinate difficulty is not the set of requirements God has to meet in order to be self-consistent but the various levels of anger and inner conflict that prevent us being at home with ourselves (being still, being able to bear our own gaze, being able to bear our own powerlessness or whatever), Julian's is both a consoling and a significantly demanding theology. Its 'problems' can be resolved only by the erosion of my anger, my refusal of life.

'Sinne is no dede': what we call sin is the refusal to act humanly: it is to allow my action to be fatally invaded by the 'contrariousness' that comes with the fallen state of Adam's children. Adam falls because he is in haste to do God's will: that is, he falls because, in spite of everything, he is at some level relying on the intensity of his own labour to do justice to what God desires and commands. When he is weighed down and immobilised as a result of his fall, he is confused not only about what he thinks or believes but about what he feels about or for God. Shame and fear generate that internal anger which is then projected on to God in the mistrustfulness that Julian describes, for example, in chapter lxxii. And this confusion is clearly one of the factors that produce the theological tangles Julian is determined to deconstruct. God, meanwhile, is not only unchanged but refuses to ascribe the servant's fall to ill-will or rebellion; he is eternally free to be who he is and to enact who/what he is, and so his sustaining presence in the centre of the world's life – and thus of the human agent – cannot alter and needs no conditions to be 'satisfied'. What we contribute to the whole picture is, tragically, those forms of refusal which erode real agency. Sin may look like action, but in fact it is failure to act: it is thus as opposite to God as could be (lxxii); yet at the same time, simply because it is not truly *action*, it cannot change what we are any more than it can change what God is. All real action is implicitly a relating to, even a 'beholding of' God, so that we can say, counter-intuitively, that at the most fundamental level of our existence we simply see God – because we are the active presence of his truth and wisdom insofar as we live at all (xliv). And it is this deep level of natural 'beholding' and desiring to be what we are (the continuation in us of God's 'desiring' to be what he is, God's loving self-contemplation) that we seek to access or activate in prayer (xli–xliii, xlvii, lxvii, etc.). Anti-theology becomes specific and practical, as it were, by this entry into the centre of what we are, into

God's dwelling-place, the 'homeliest home' of Christ in the heart (lxviii). The inevitability of sin (lxxix), even its 'behovely' quality (xxvii), its 'appropriateness', as we might translate it,[11] has something to do with our need to be aware of our radical instability: we are created participants in God's act, but precisely as *created* participants we are capable over time of falling away from action into the nothingness of our self-oriented anxieties.

We could paraphrase Julian by saying that grace is God's 'no' to our 'no': our persistent leaning towards nothingness, to the refusal of the act that is our very being, is what is annihilated by openness to God. The language of annihilation, mentioned earlier, is dangerous; it can be heard as recommending some sort of cancellation of creation itself, the 'de-creation' that we meet in some of Simone Weil's writing, for example. But Julian's concern is different: what de-creates is the fact of sin; but sin is specifically and emphatically what does not define me (or any other creature). Repeatedly she insists that our nature is held together in its completeness in and by God's action, so that our fallenness does not destroy what we are (liii, lvii, for example). God's nature and God's grace belong together, and we can understand God's grace as simply the mode in which divine nature sustains created nature: 'grace was sent out to save kinde, and kepe kinde, and destroy sinne, and bring again fair kinde into the blessed point from thens it came'; and 'grace is God, as unmade kinde is God. He is two in manner werking, and one in love' (lxiii). However drastically and disastrously we refuse to 'enact' God, there is always divine action at work within us, not consenting to this lack of consent. When we say 'no', there is an abiding 'no' to this 'no' at the heart of what we are. And, to connect this again with our theme of anti-theology, when our theology in effect ends up saying 'no' to God, 'no' to the indestructible affirmation that is God's eternal work, the work itself continues without interruption to refuse our refusal.

Yet this does not leave us with a bland doctrine of the natural goodness of our nature, let alone the non-seriousness of the fall – the picture, complete with pet cat, that has made Julian a favourite with some contemporaries who dislike the language of original sin or fallenness and think of her as some kind of precursor of a 'creation' spirituality. Clifton Wolters's strange judgement[12] that she 'might never have seen really malevolent evil in others' expresses the kind of misreading to which she has too often been subjected. But Julian's visions, after all, begin with the sight of Jesus's anguish, evoked in unsparing detail; the eighth vision insists strongly on the drawn-out process of his dying ('as if he had be sennight deade, dying, at the point of outpassing, alwey suffering the gret paine', xvi). Sustaining God's 'no' to our 'no' is more costly than we can imagine for the incarnate Christ, the human embodiment of God's faithful presence among us. The force of our refusal is reflected in the protracted agony of Christ's dying, so that we cannot conceive of God's faithfulness without this image of a long-drawn-out death agony. Julian constantly draws us back to recognising – in a classically Augustinian way – that if sin is an absence of action or reality, this most definitely doesn't mean that it is illusory or without effect. Our refusal to act humanly (which is also to act 'divinely', acting in continuity with the eternal act of love or gift) is hideously damaging to ourselves and to the divine embodiment in Jesus: Julian

180

depicts that damage both in the evocation of Christ's suffering and in her eloquence about the unnatural character of sin (e.g. lxiii, 'sinne is ... contrarious to our fair kinde', and thus fouler than hell itself).

It's worth noting that Julian's approach here has a lot in common with the understanding of Christ's death developed by the late Sebastian Moore in his extraordinary book *The Crucified is no Stranger*[13] – a contemporary instance of 'anti-theology' if ever there was one: 'the point that theologians describe as mysterious is embarrassingly simple',[14] because theologians are always being drawn into thinking of the cross as something directed towards God (to make something possible for God), whereas it is in fact directed towards us (to make something possible for us). And it is precisely in the urge to see the cross as propitiating God, making a difference to God, that we do violence to ourselves: clinging to ourselves and refusing to be what in God's eyes we are (yes, the echo of Hopkins is deliberate) is piling the violence of denial on top of our nature. We can see this only as and when we see it as an endlessly prolonged putting-to-death of God in the flesh, putting to death the one agent who lives outside and beyond the fear of death, who denies our fearful denials of death.[15] We are compulsively trying, says Moore, to deny that there is a level of reality at which denying death is itself denied, so that death ceases to dictate to us (and to push us into the self-absorption of fear). As he admits, language buckles under the strain of all these double negatives; but the point is indeed simple. The death of Christ is our human refusal both of God and of what we are; and it is at the same time the divine refusal of our denials. As divine and human, Christ can embody the consequence of refusing God and ourselves – the ultimate murder of the innocent – and can also embody the indestructible faithfulness of God in the midst of human self-destruction. 'We have to think of a God closer to our evil than we ever dare to be. We have to think of him not as standing at the end of the way we take when we run away from our evil in the search for good, but as taking hold of us in our evil, at the sore point which the whole idealistic thrust of man is concerned to avoid.'[16]

This follows Julian closely, though in a very different idiom. The fundamental concern in both is the unbroken relation of God to what Julian calls 'kinde', the fact of grace as something always already done, offered, enacted, so that there is no need to make something possible for God by a complex transaction, only for us to be freed to receive what we are from God's hand. And in the last part of this reflection, I want briefly to look at what this means for our practice of prayer. Julian is regularly bracketed with the great contemplative teachers of her age, not least with the author of *The Cloud of Unknowing*; but anyone looking to Julian for the same kind of practical advice is likely to be puzzled. There are ideas and images here which provide deeply fruitful themes for meditation, we might say; but has she anything to tell us about the nature and disciplines of contemplative life?

The answer is in the very character of her 'anti-theology', not in any specific counsel on what to do in prayer. If the difficulty of reconciliation with God's truth lies in us, not in God, then the work of contemplation must be framed in the kind of self-examination that helps us see how we are refusing what is there. We need to keep the habits of our imagination under quiet scrutiny, so

that those movements of the mind which project on to
God the turmoil of our own insides are brought into the
light. When anger or craving arises, when resentment
or the sense of powerlessness or fear surface, we need
to be able to see these things as the disturbance of our
true life as it is held in the eternal Trinity – and not to
create dramas in the life of God, divine difficulties which
must somehow be overcome. If we are able to isolate
and identify these movements, we shall be more free to
acknowledge the faithful presence that is simply there in
and for us. Gazing at and reflecting on the suffering of
Christ is not, for Julian, a means of generating self-lacer-
ating emotion but recognising the logic of my denials of
life: I am involved, in all sorts of ways, in avoiding love,
and love's avoidance is the drawn-out putting-to-death
of God and God in me. Yet it is at the same time the
reminder that God cannot be put to death and that the
passion of Christ also declares the unchanging presence
of God in the centre of our being.

Thus we are pointed back into the single crucial recognition: God is already acting, in my very being and in
every act of mine that is open to his action. Hence the
famous statement that Christ is 'grounde of thy beseking'
(xli) is a natural implication of Julian's general conviction
about action, divine and human. In prayer, we confront
or apprehend ('experience' is, as usual, a misleading and
wrong word) the bare fact of God's faithful thereness
along with the uneven course of our created activity,
most particularly the unevenness of our trust that God
is present and responding. What we may be sure of is
that God 'hears' simply because there is no difference,
certainly no *distance* between God's presence and act in
us and God's being in himself. This is why we can say

that God's merciful answering of prayer is nothing to do with our intensity of address to him, but is rooted in his 'proper goodnesse' (xli; and compare chapter vi, 'the goodness of God is the highest prayer'). As in other contexts, we find in this chapter a further dismantling of theological convention: Christ receives our prayer and brings it to the Father, which is straightforward and scriptural enough; but two fresh themes are strongly underlined. The first is simply that there can be no sense in which our prayer *causes* any act or disposition on God's part: once we recognise 'theyse swete words ther he seyeth, "I am ground"', and grasp that our praying is already his action, we shall do more rather than less of it, simply because we now see how inseparable our action is from God's. We shall neither struggle to keep up with divine demands, with the requirement to exert our finite efforts so as to bring about infinite action, nor sink back in despair at the impossibility of the task. And the second new perspective offered by Julian is to insist on Christ's thankfulness for our prayer – another potentially startling reversal. But what chapter xli seems to be arguing is that if prayer is the flowering of divine action in us and through us, God will delight in it simply because God delights in being God; the joy with which the eternal Son stores our prayer 'in tresure' in heaven is the divine joy in the sight of divine life being lived in the finite order. The bold language of Christ being 'grateful' for our prayer underscores this point: while there is an obvious and fundamental sense in which Julian's logic forbids any alteration in God as a result of what is happening in the world, we can stretch a point in saying that the augmentation of God's joy through the joy of created beings means that the divine perfection is 'augmented' not by an increase in its eternal reality but by its reflection and participation in the world. It is another of Julian's Augustinian moments, recalling some of the arguments of Augustine in the *De doctrina Christiana* about how God loves us with a love of 'use', not 'enjoyment' (which on the face of it seems to contradict Julian), in the sense that every expression of God's love towards us is being used by God to bring about not his increased bliss or fulfilment but ours.[17]

So prayer for Julian is bound up with self-awareness, a keen eye for what is getting in the way of God's active being in us; and it will flourish as and when we stop trying to pray in order to make something happen on God's part and so become more fully aligned with the simple 'happening of God' which is going on unbrokenly in all reality. The stilling of our activity and the focus of attention on what is, not on what we are bringing about – this is the prayer Julian implicitly commends to us. The exercise in what I have been calling 'anti-theology' is, throughout the *Revelation*, directed towards this; it is a mistake to think (as one or two commentators seem to) that when she writes explicitly about prayer she is simply bolting on a dutiful bundle of routine exhortations to a record of exciting visionary or 'mystical' experiences. What she sees is consistently something (someone) who persuades us to wonder, 'Am I asking the right questions where God is concerned?' 'Revelation' is a therapy for theological language: it is the process whereby we come to grasp how many of our theological problems are about the unreflective projecting on to God of tensions and dead-ends generated in our own hearts by our own fears. What Julian sees is, indeed, like the poetic moment evoked by Hill and Eliot: *this* is where the language folds in to itself, folds in to its own solid integrity, becomes 'at one with itself': where certain crucially dangerous dualities are set aside so that the one act of God in the diversity of created performances may simply happen. Julian, as I have said, is not attacking doctrinal formulation as such, let alone adopting a facile anti-intellectual or anti-conceptual stance. But she is inviting us to look carefully at our formulations: do they or don't they embody the fundamental and unifying content of revelation in Christ? Do they generate anxious intellectual games and spiritual self-harm? Do they ultimately point to the single mystery of an infinite act of shared joy? Dealing with such questions obliges us to come to terms with the starkest of images, the vision not only of the crucified in the most direct form but of an immeasurably prolonged putting-to-death of the life that is in us as it is embodied once and for all in Jesus. No alibis there, no resignation to a passive position; but no obsessive self-abasement either. We are invited, soberly and quietly, to see what we are in seeing the dying Christ. But in seeing the dying Christ, we also see how and why the love that holds us in being is indestructible. 'I never lefte my hands of my workes' (xi); 'I it am that thou meneste. I it am that is alle' (xxvi).

'Arte thou well apaide?' asks Jesus; and Julian replies, 'Ye, good lorde, gramercy.' Her anti-theology has silenced those dramas in which we imagine the travails of a God trapped as we are trapped; and theology is allowed again to discover the dense singularity of simplicity, the simplicity of 'thy lords mening in this thing'.

13

'Know Thyself': What Kind of an Injunction?

To be told, 'Know thyself', is to be told that I don't know myself *yet*: it carries the assumption that I am in some sense distracted from what or who I actually am, that I am in error or at least ignorance about myself. It thus further suggests that my habitual stresses, confusions and frustrations are substantially the result of failure or inability to see what is most profoundly true of me: the complex character of my injuries or traumas, the distinctive potential given me by my history and temperament. I conceal my true feelings from my knowing self; I am content to accept the ways in which other people define me, and so fail to 'take my own authority' and decide for myself who or what I shall be. The therapy-orientated culture of the North Atlantic world in the past couple of decades has increasingly taken this picture as foundational, looking to 'self-discovery' or 'self-realisation' as the precondition of moral and mental welfare. And the sense of individual alienation from a true and authoritative selfhood mirrors the political struggle for the right of hitherto disadvantaged groups, especially non-white and non-male, to establish their own self-definition. The rhetoric of discovering a true but buried identity spreads over both private and political spheres. The slogan of the earliest generation of articulate feminists, 'The personal is the political', expresses the recognition of how this connection might be made.

R. D. Laing's seminal work of 1960, *The Divided Self*, did much to popularise the idea of a distinction between different 'self-systems', with the essential feature of schizoid disorder being defined as the separation of a 'real', 'inner' self, invisible to the observer, from the behaviour of the empirical ('false') self.[1] For Laing, the clinical schizophrenic's condition is an extreme case of the schizoid fantasies common in supposedly sane persons, whose behaviour and language betray a belief that they have an untouched core of selfhood which must not be compromised or limited by involved action, but which lives in a state of fictitious freedom and omnipotence – described by Laing[2] as the direct opposite of Hegel's insistence in the *Phenomenology* that performance alone measures what is real in the life of an agent. Laing, in fact, is diagnosing the language of a 'real', non-appearing self as a sign of dysfunction; but already in *The Divided Self* and more dramatically in some of his later writings, he is also suggesting that the dysfunction is virtually forced on vast numbers of persons because the public realm of language and action is systematically oppressive and distorting.

From this aspect of Laing's thought, reinforced by his abundant use of Kafka and Sartre, it is not difficult to slip into the view that the socially constructed and socially sustained self is indeed false in some absolute sense, and that authenticity lies in a hidden dimension, a core of uncompromised interiority. This is a conclusion which Laing himself is very careful not to draw; but a superficial reading, aided by existentialist and oriental ideas (imperfectly digested), could produce the paradoxical doctrine that the 'true' self is present but inoperative, and may be discovered by bracketing out large tracts of the social, the corporate, the linguistic. This is in some respects obviously the child of the classical project of psychoanalysis, the decoding of present linguistic and symbolic behaviour so as to uncover the conflicts which generate my current self-presentation. But the important difference is that, for the searcher for the lost, 'true' self, the business of penetrating behind self-presentation leads *beyond* buried conflict to an authoritative source or centre of energy. Self-knowledge thus becomes more than an acquaintance with the history of trauma and defence, and appears as the possibility of liberating contact with a power that can transform present performance, replacing a false system of self-representation with another system which does not systematically mask real desires and needs.

This may be conceived, picking up the clues of Eastern religious philosophy, as *the* Self, the divine undifferentiated reality within; or as an individual system of immanent forces in balance, a temperamental pattern of gifts, characteristic affective responses, undistorted desires. It is, in either case, habitually pictured as present but concealed. The archaeology of analysis reveals, eventually, a living subject with an agenda distinct from what has been the agenda of habitual self-awareness. From one point of view, this scheme represents a quite remarkable rearguard action fought by romanticism against the dissolution of the autonomous agent threatened by analytic disciplines—remarkable because it leads analysis inexorably back towards a pre-Freudian mythology of unambiguous nature, the naked self, prior to history and conversation.

The philosophical problems of this naked self are tediously familiar. In this particular context, we should have to ask: how can a present discourse, shaped by the history of my speaking and hearing, intelligibly claim to re-establish what is not so shaped? How could such a claim be tested? What sense can we make of the idea of a self with specific dispositions and desires prior to relationships if the self is self-aware only against the presence of a resisting or interrupting other? The archaeological analogy is question-begging (how does the compromised active self recognise what it discovers as its own truer reality?): the 'discovered' self is surely the construct of present actions and interactions—an insight authoritatively mapped by Jacques Lacan in all its complex ramifications.[3] For Lacan, self-knowledge is precisely a recognition of the dialectical nature of being a 'subject', the inescapable involvement of the self in the desire of the other: it is, in the analytical encounter of the present moment (in which the self is confronted by another self – the analyst – trained, as far as possible, to set aside the ego-system obsessed with the meeting of desires), the recognition that the ego conceals the way in which the subject fundamentally exists – as lack, as the wanting of what it is not, and thus both relational and self-cancelling.[4]

If there is a secret to be uncovered, it is that there is nothing prior to reciprocity. The way in which the ego habitually organises itself is as a system potentially or really *in possession* of what it desires: but the subject is constituted as that which does not possess, desiring and desiring to be desired. Self-knowledge delivers not a hidden, authentic agenda to replace our current troubled system of self-representation, but a sense of one's irreversible engagement in an exchange with no substantial fixed points: it locates us more firmly now in the complexities of exchange, and teaches us not what we must do to be true to our 'nature', but simply to be endlessly iconoclastic about the claims of the ego. Self-knowledge amounts to a practice of conversational self-questioning, and the 'true' self is no substance but simply the enacting of such a practice. The ego, of course, is never simply removed or dissolved: its formation is a primordial and (again) irreversible misunderstanding of what the subject is, and so it is what makes self-questioning both possible and necessary. I am indeed alienated from truth, and the substantive 'I' is the sign of that recognition; but this does not mean an apotheosis of instinctual existence or an attempt to dissolve historical consciousness (despite the vitriolic criticisms of Luc Ferry and Alain Renaut on this point).[5] Conscious life is what is set up by the tension between subject and ego: truthful consciousness acknowledges this and understands that the subject's presence in history and language depends on the false concreteness of the ego (demands and gratifications, goals and fulfilments), *and* that these fixities are constantly being subverted, *and* that the very *movement* of speech depends in turn on this subversion.

Lacan is worth pondering because he presents almost an inversion of romanticism and the Sartrean pathos of the frustrated true self. The hidden and uncorrupted subjectivity that is somehow present as a realm into which I can escape is the most fundamental of all misunderstandings, because there is no desire which is not already mediated – i.e. in some sense alienated. My 'I' is given, learned from the other; beyond it stands not a coherent and unified selfhood but – for Lacan – something like a foundational absence, a state of death. The subject's quest for itself is for him a desire for death. Yet this shocking recognition enables the recognition that the 'satisfaction' of the subject is not after all intrinsically at odds with the satisfaction of all subjects. The analytical conversation lays bare the fraudulence of the ego; the analyst's minimal ego enables the analysand's ego to be relativised, and intersubjectivity to appear, the reciprocal recognition of subjects.[6]

The unclarities and points of strain in Lacan have been amply discussed, and I have no intention of simply presenting his account as incontrovertible truth (I find the status of the subject as primordial absence and Lacan's thesis about the subject's fulfilment in death especially problematic: René Girard's critique[7] of Lacan on this point is pertinent, arguing that Lacan is still not free from the mythology of pre-cultural desire and primary self-constitution). But in so far as Lacan offers a uniquely full and acute critique of the Hegelian 'noble soul' as the terminus of self-knowledge, he makes it clear that, if self-knowledge is liberative, it is not because it issues in an authoritatively self-defining subject. The point applies politically as well as psychologically, and must stand as a question to (for example) essentialist and archaeological discourse within feminism.

But the purpose of this essay is to look at the rhetoric of self-knowledge in the religious context; and since the language of 'true selfhood' and certain techniques of self-examination and self-appraisal, loosely grounded in psychoanalytical theory, are enjoying extremely wide currency in literature about Christian spirituality,[8] it seems as well to begin with some general reminders of the current difficulties in a discussion of self-knowledge. What I propose to do in the rest of this paper is to look briefly at three ways in which the injunction to self-knowledge has been used in Christian tradition, so as to pose two questions: first, are the traditional usages vulnerable to the critique of a post-Lacanian (and post-Wittgensteinian) account of the self? and second, does the contemporary Christian interest in self-knowledge belong in the same frame of reference as the language of earlier writers? My tentative conclusion will be that the answer to both these questions is 'No', and that some aspects of earlier Christian language about self-knowledge leave open the possibility of a useful conversation with the recent discussion I've mentioned.

My first example is the rhetoric of self-knowledge and self-recognition in the Christian gnostic literature of the second and third Christian centuries, in particular some of the texts from the Nag Hammadi collection. Fundamental to the mythology of all groups using gnostic idiom is the belief that our present human condition is enslaved by forgetfulness of our origin. Thus the *Apocryphon of John*[9] describes how the ignorant world creator, himself oblivious of his origins, is tricked into imparting some element of divine spirit to the primordial human subject, who thus excites the jealousy of the cosmic powers who imprison this subject in matter and mortality, 'the bond of forgetfulness'. Adam is placed in Eden and told to eat and drink and enjoy himself.[10] Divine grace hides in Adam the saving element of *epinoia*, intellectual grasp, but this has to be activated by a saviour who is first and foremost 'remembrance' (p. 115). The *Gospel of Truth*[11] accordingly describes the one who is saved from the wreckage of the cosmos as one who 'knows where he comes from and where he is going to' (p. 40). The sayings of Jesus in the *Gospel of Thomas*[12] echo this frequently, but strikingly turn on the idea that the 'hidden' truth of who we are is in fact plain and obvious. 'If those who lead you say to you, "See the Kingdom is in the sky, then the birds of the sky will precede you ... The Kingdom is inside of you, and it is outside of you. When you come to know yourselves, then you will become known ... Recognise what is in your sight"';[13] 'What you look forward to has already come, but you do not recognise it';[14] 'The Kingdom of the Father is spread out upon the earth, and men do not see it'.[15]

Examples could be multiplied, but the sense conveyed is clear. As in the Greek mysteries in which the original *gnōthi sauton* had its setting,[16] I must recognise what *kind* of a being I fundamentally am: self-knowledge here is nothing to do with individual self-analysis, a particular history, but is the discovery of the history I share with all the children of light – a pre-history, rather, in which all that constitutes particular history is the creation of a cosmic *ressentiment*. I have *lost* nothing in being subjected to the indignity of incarnation, but I am separated from my true self and my true home by forces external to myself who have 'clothed' me in a false identity (hence the significance in *Thomas* of the metaphor of stripping, as in Saying 37).[17] *Thomas* presents the most sophisticated treatment of the theme, in suggesting that enlightenment is not simply knowing the myth of your origins and destiny, but understanding that the state of the world before your eyes tells you the truth of your nature: you are the seer, not the seen, and the material world lies before you, passive, like a corpse (Sayings 56 and 80).[18] Understand that you understand, that you are not bound by reaction to what is before you, and you understand that you occupy a place beyond all worldly schemes of differentiation. You are the light in which things are seen. Where is the place where Jesus stands? It is the place from which light emanates, the interior of the enlightened person (Saying 24).[19]

What we must recognize, then, is that our 'real' life is undifferentiated, a sort of Aristotelean self-noesis, indistinguishable perhaps from the life of what *Thomas* calls 'the All'. Gnostic self-recognition certainly deploys a rhetoric that has affinities with the romantic model of the buried, authentic self; but the buried self here is not the touchstone of authentic desire or unillusioned action, merely the purity of intellectual self-presence. In one way – unsurprisingly? – this veers towards the Buddhist ideal of self-knowledge, the dismantling of all specific desires, properties or projects so as to perceive the underlying absence of anything but the sheer 'thereness' of the empty abundance that is both blissful fulfilment and contentless void (*nirvāṇa* and *śūnyatā*). At another level, the analogies with a Lacanian analysis are striking, especially in the virtual dismissal of habitual bodily and emotional self-presentation as the effect of 'captivity' or falsehood, and the ultimate identification of the subject as absence. The difference, though, is at least twofold: the gnostic subject may be an absence, but could not be called a *lack*; it is beyond desire, and so beyond history. And the intersubjectivity that can be created in the analytic encounter is no part of the gnostic hope, which looks to a recovery of non-differentiation, a divine sameness. From yet another perspective, however, gnostic rhetoric is indeed the distant parent of romantic mythology, in constructing not simply a picture of a world of error or misprision, but an actively hostile environment deliberately stifling the truth out of envy. The false and forgetful self is in no sense (as it would be for the Buddhist or the Lacanian) the formation, the *responsibility*, of the subject: it is wholly the creation of a hostile power. The forgotten self acquires the pathos of a victim – a move which decisively politicises the language of gnosticism, giving the self a project of struggle against not alienated but nakedly alien force (though, once again, a document like *Thomas* shows how this language in turn can be demythologised and freed from the crude rhetoric of struggle against something external).

Gnosticism's difficulty is always in this last aspect of its schema. If history and the body are indeed *radically* alien to the spirit, the spirit is a stranger to guilt and division: it is not self-alienated but forcibly disguised from itself. Whence then comes the division? The problem is pushed back into the realm of the divine life itself, and there the same problems recur. Divine self-alienation (myths of the fall of Sophia) is no easier to theorise, and perhaps the only consistent solution to such a problematic was the absolute dualism of the Manichees. The rhetoric of gnostic self-knowledge represents a drastic working-through of certain features in the earliest Christian language we can trace – the summons to see one's ordinary self-presentation as deceitful (as in the synoptic Jesus's sharp antitheses between what is visible and what is 'in the heart' – Matthew 5.21ff. – or the Johannine Jesus's allusions to the blindness of those who claim they can see – John 9.39–41 – or Paul's regular opposition of 'flesh' and 'spirit' as moral systems); what it shows, though, certainly to the majority of writers in what was to become the Christian mainstream, is that to render the problem of self-deceit in such a way as to disclaim ownership of one's own deceptive history is to set up a problem as serious for metaphysics as for individual psychology.[20] The isolation of the non-responsible, inactive and impassive self finally requires the postulating, at one and the same time, of an inactive and impassive God and a universe of uncontrollably delusory systems.

Thus the relentless elaboration of the theme of self-deceit alone leads to the vision of a reality eternally and irreparably – and unintelligibly – split, and to something like a technically schizoid construction of the world of the subject. A truth that is strictly incommunicable in habitual (bodily/temporal) self-presentation is liberative only negatively, as a relativising of *all* determinations: it does not modify our negotiating of *particular* determinations. Consequently, as Christian language develops, the idea of an independent spiritual core to the person, a self untouched by time and guilt, recedes further and further: even with the pre-existent *nous* of Origen's anthropology, the present state of the self is intimately connected with the free self-determination of this primordial subject, which both is and is not involved in time and matter. The destiny of the spiritual subject is liberation, but to arrive there I must learn virtue *in* the school of the fallen soul and the empirical body. The *nous* is in principle independent of the body, yet it can only become what it should be – a spirit uninterruptedly contemplating God – through the life of material and temporal selfhood.

The difference between the language of gnostic ethics and spirituality and what finally became the normative

idiom of Catholic Christianity is very clear if we turn to a
second brief case-study, the discussion of self-knowledge
in St Bernard's homilies on the Song of Songs.[21] Sermons
35 to 37 in particular deal with a text from the first
chapter of the Canticle in the Vulgate, *si ignoras te ...
egredere* (Song of Songs 1.7): the Bride is told that if
she fails to know herself, she must leave the sweets of
contemplation for the exile of a life dominated by grati-
fying the needs of the senses. This, of course, is what the
fate of Adam was; and why does Adam fall? By misunderstanding the meaning of his human dignity (35.6).
He forgets that he is a creature (and thus dependent on
God), and is expelled from Eden, thus becoming subject
to a second and more serious ignorance of himself,
forgetfulness of his rational and spiritual nature (35.7).
Not knowing oneself, then, and not knowing God are
intimately connected: if I do not know that I am God's
creature, because I am hypnotised by the grandeur of the
intellectual gifts given me, I shall not in fact know how
to exercise those gifts, and I shall cease to be a rational
creature at all (this rests on Bernard's general belief that,
since reason in us is God's image, it cannot function when
it does not have God for its object). Faulty self-knowledge has thus led to our present sad plight: what, then,
does it mean to know myself truthfully now? It is to see
my helplessness and loss, to discover that I now live 'in
a region where likeness to God has been forfeited' (*regio
dissimilitudinis*, 36.5). Yet simultaneously I must know
that God continues to hear me and to give me grace: if
I see myself as a fallen sinner, I must also see myself as a
graced sinner, since I could not truthfully know my sin
without knowing God (I couldn't know what it was like
to lose the image of God if I had no awareness of God).

'Your self-knowledge will be a step to the knowledge of God; he will become visible to you according as his image is being renewed within you' (36.6). Self-knowledge thus becomes the condition for repentance, prayer and practical charity (37.2): the Spirit of God begins to realise in us the dignity of God's children by forming us in holiness. So by our penitent recognition of what we are, we 'sow in tears'; but God's mercy guarantees that we 'reap in joy' (37.4, quoting Ps. 125.5).

This is quite a complex depiction of self-knowledge. If we had to identify its focal themes, we could say that they are firstly the need throughout for a recognition that we are constituted 'rational' or 'spiritual' or whatever in virtue of relation to the creator, not as self-sufficient individualities, and secondly the priority here and now of recognising fallibility and failure as the self's truth, while perceiving also that such a judgement presupposes relation to God even in the acknowledgement that no proper relation yet exists. Thus there is no selfhood prior to the address or gift of God: reason responds to this, rather than having a simple primacy or autonomy. Even as a Godless and forgetful sinner, I am called into being as a self by the prior love of God. Self-knowledge makes no sense except as achieved in the face of God, in the light of God, and truthful self-knowledge establishes itself as such by incorporating recognition of the divine love; this is as true for Adam in paradise as for us now. The 'authentic' self is what I acknowledge as already, non-negotiably, caught up in a continuing encounter with or response to divine action; and the acknowledgement is inseparable from converted behaviour. The person who knows him- or herself is manifest as such in the practice of prayer and almsgiving. Or, in short, the meaning of self-knowledge here is displayed in the performing of acts intelligible as the acts of a finite being responding to an initiative of generosity from beyond itself, an initiative wholly unconditioned by any past history on the self's part of oblivion or betrayal.

This is a model very nearly at the opposite pole from that of gnostic language. What to the gnostic is the terminus of the search for a true identity is here, in effect, the most lethal of errors: we do not arrive at a subject functionally identical with the worldless divinity, essentially indeterminate, but at a point of primitive determination, an irreducible status as hearer and recipient. The capacity to make sense of the world follows not from identity with the light of reason or order beyond the contingent present, but from grasping one's own contingency, articulating dependence (reason *as imago dei*). Identifying the substance of the self with a non-relational intellectual power is the pride which exiles us from Eden, and constantly pulls us to the sub-rational level of serving pure appetite (which we may successfully disguise as reasoning). Furthermore, our condition is historical, in the sense that, since there is no essence prior to relation with God to which we can have recourse, we are always what we have made of ourselves in our encounter with God – not imprisoned angels, but struggling and inept conversationalists, whose errors and self-delusions build themselves into a formidable carapace of unreality, reinforced by every fresh stage in our self-representation unless interrupted by awareness of God – which is necessarily a silencing of our self-projecting. Thus there can be no authentic *image* of the self that has definition and fixity of itself (which would be another projection of the falsity of Adam's original misperception) – there is the recognition of a history of error and failure to respond to what I now see or hear afresh (God), and the adoption of the kind of practice that militates against error about my metaphysical status – prayer and charity. There can be no *ressentiment* against the cosmos, since the imprisoning illusion is self-generated – reason's attempt to reflect on itself without the mediation of God's creating love. If there is a 'politics' to this account of self-knowing, it is not based on a rhetoric of reclaiming what has been taken away, or identifying a guiltless and uninvolved victim at the centre of my identity, but is orientated rather towards the suspicion of claims for the finality of self-definition, reasoned defences of the pursuit of interest and appetite on the part of a pseudo-self (individual or collective?) denying its contingency. The mistaken subject here is constructed as possessing, not lacking, power in the world of negotiation, and needing to recover a fundamental perception of *limited* power rather than a primordial liberty. That there is an ambivalence to this also is evident; more of that later.

Bernard's theology is decisively shaped by the heritage of Augustinianism, and it is to Augustine himself that we turn for a third and final perspective on the language of self-knowledge. The *Confessions* is a work permeated on practically every page by the acknowledgement that true knowledge of self is inseparable from true knowledge of God. *Cognoscam te Domine cognitor meus*, writes Augustine at the beginning of Book X, and, a little later (X. 5), *quod de me scio, te mihi lucente scio.* As Book VII in particular makes clear, the recognition of God's absolute transcendence is a crucial moment in liberating Augustine from a crude and sterile picture of the self and its moral world: the problem of evil is reconceived as a problem of the variability of the will in a contingent environment, rather than a question of how a substantial alien force could intrude itself into the world's fixed territory; the mind's evaluating and connection-making activities are seen as intelligible only if they take for granted an independent (non-worldly) measure of value and coherence. It is the utter and irreducible difference between God and the human mind that frees the mind to recognise itself and to be itself – to know that it is not a sort of material object, but is simply the activity of making sense of the world and of its own history: memory, says Augustine (X. 17), *animus est et hoc ego ipse sum*. I 'am' the recollecting and ordering of my past.[22] This is, by definition, an endless labour, and it can be carried forward only in the belief that there exists a full and just perspective on my history, not dependent on my own fallible perception. Truthful self-knowledge thus entails a constantly self-critical autobiographical project, striving to construct the narrative least unfaithful to the divine perspective. It will, of course, never *be* the divine perspective, because what God *sees,* I *learn* (and constantly, with every new action, must relearn). *Confessions* X describes vividly how the present awareness of what distorts judgement and desire enforces humility and a certain provisionality in our accounts of ourselves: what we can be certain of is not our own perseverance but the mercy of God, who alone sees what we are and what we need.

Some of these themes recur in the masterwork of Augustine's maturity, the *de trinitate,* whose eighth to tenth books are very largely devoted to a complex and subtle discussion of self-knowing. A full treatment would be difficult in the space available here,[23] but the salient points are these. Self-knowledge and self-love are brought into close connection, because of the recognition that the self is in motion to the Good (or at least what it thinks is the Good), that it cannot avoid making judgements of approbation and disapprobation: the self operates as if it knew more or less what it *wanted to be like* (*de trin.* VIII.iii–vi). We love good people, and part of what we love in them is their own love, their will that goodness be accessible to all (VIII. viii). So to know ourselves is to recognise our involvement in moral process by way of desire: we want to be just and loving, we learn justice and love from the just love of good people, and so we must understand ourselves to be so constituted as to be in love with loving (and so, ultimately, with the unreserved generosity of God). Book IX spells out some implications: we can't love ourselves without knowing ourselves, but we can't know without desire (IX.ii–vii). Consequently, in Book X, the paradox is stated in full force: 'total' self-knowledge is precisely the knowledge of the self as incomplete, as seeking (X.iii). Because it makes no sense to split the mind into the bit that knows and the bit that is known, then if I know myself as questioning and incomplete, as wanting to know, I know all I can know of what I am (X.iv). I know, very importantly, that I am neither God nor beast: a creature, but a reasoning creature (X.v: here is the theme of self-knowledge as knowing one's place in the order of things, which is found elsewhere in Augustine, and is obviously seminal for Bernard). I know too that my mind cannot be a material object, cannot be comparable to one of the things I think about (X.ix–x), because knowing the mind is always knowing from within a fluid activity, not a fixed external object.

I have tried to argue elsewhere[24] that Augustine's account here of the indubitability of self-knowledge may be closer to Wittgenstein's *On Certainty* than to Descartes, since it is above all an attempt to show that knowing the self is something quite distinct from any processes of 'coming to know' in which questions of evidence and relative degree of certainty can properly be raised (you couldn't be *fairly* sure you knew yourself on Augustine's account). Its most significant contribution to our present discussion, though, is the insistence upon the *unfinishable* nature of self-knowledge (a theme that can be paralleled, incidentally, in the Christian East, particularly in Gregory of Nyssa).[25] The self is in construction; the relating of a history is not the fixing of the self's definition or the uncovering of a hidden truth, but part of the process of construction, a holding operation. Furthermore, the process is bound up with the desire for the Good, for *iustitia*: the self in construction is a self whose good is understood in terms of a universally shareable good, and the self is not known adequately without a grasp of the inseparability of its good from the good of all. If there is a 'secret' to be uncovered by the search for self-knowledge, it is perhaps this unconscious involvement in desire for the common good; and if there is a 'politics' of self-knowledge in Augustine, it lies in the dissolution of any fantasy that the good can be definitively possessed in history by any individual or any determinate group in isolation. The distance between God as *summum bonum* and all creatures means both that there can be no settled state of absolute good for this world, and that there is (effectively) unlimited time for the working and reworking of corporate movement towards the Good.[26]

It is time now to attempt some drawing together of the threads of this diffuse discussion. I have suggested that the rejection of gnostic language about the hidden self left 'mainstream' Christianity with the task of dealing with its own fundamental vocabulary of self-deception and restoration without endorsing the mythology of a supra-historical subject, a self prior to and untouched by a history of interrelation and of determination by that interrelatedness. Bernard and Augustine present us with a self constructed in and only in contingency, and intelligible only as responding to address from beyond itself, never self-creating. For Bernard, if we do not see our rationality as tending God-wards, we become sub-rational: we need a de-mystifying of our intellectual and spiritual powers and an acquaintance with our power-lessness to avoid error, left to ourselves. For Augustine, we need to come to terms fully with our finitude and to recognise that our rationality is always enmeshed in desire – most primitively, that desire for the good or the just that is obscured by our habitual misidentifica-tion of what we want, which results from the fictions of rivalry that corrupt the common life of human beings and reinforce an image of the self as an atomistic subject orientated to an endless series of specific grat-ifications (a consumer, in fact). For both Bernard and Augustine, the inaccessibility of the divine perspective is paradoxically liberating: there is always a resource for the renewal or conversion or enlargement of myself independent of what may happen to be my resources at any given moment, and there is always the possibility of more adequately ordering the telling of my life as I draw towards a perspective on myself undistorted by my self-interest – a perspective never possessed, never simply mine, but imaginable as a horizon against which other perspectives may be tested. And none of this would be conceivable if God were the occupier of a 'point of view' comparable to my own, a positional perspective like that of an ordinary subject, only larger.

There may, then, be a convergence of sorts with the picture outlined at the beginning of this paper. Self-knowledge is a practice of criticism, specifically the criticism of the way the subject distorts its self-perception into fixity by fixation upon the meeting of needs in the determinate form in which they are mediated to us in the perception of the Other; and the ego-less interlocutor whose non-intervening presence exposes to us the possibility of this critical practice is identified as one who holds not even a residual position in the world where desires are negotiated. Theology's query to the Lacanian analytic project might be whether anything short of this horizon (of the essential absence from the world of the liberating interlocutor) enables us fully to see the possibility of a state of non-rivalry among human claims for satisfaction.[27] Theology also assumes, however, that the subject's unthematised desire to return to itself is not a desire for a 'foundational absence', for death, but for a mindful standing in its basic position of creatureliness (unfoundedness in oneself), a standing before what always precedes it: neither the birth orifice nor the phallus, as in Lacan's orthodox Freudian idiom, but the intelligible Word that precedes even biology. Lacan's own regular advertence to the religious reper-toire of images, Christian, Jewish and oriental, suggests that this parting of the ways is not a simple matter of one party taking a rationalist option for the clarities of natural science. There is more to be said from both sides.

I have hinted at a further convergence. Lacanian analysis goes a long way to removing the pathos of the victim from the destiny of the self, and Bernard and Augustine concur. But does this mean that the injunction to self-knowledge is primarily addressed to those who must be dispossessed? Both feminist and black theologies have often interpreted the summons to repentance, provisionality, the unmasking of pride, as inappropriate as addressed to them, as ideological commendations of passivity in an intolerable situation. The point is significant. We noted earlier the ambivalence of Bernard, if read as the language of the powerful (the male clerical ideologue) to the powerless – though we should remember that he is addressing male intellectual/contemplative hearers in the first instance. It is proper that any rhetoric of humility and dispossession should be subjected to suspicion. But this does not wholly turn aside the force of the Augustinian/Bernardine commendation. The style of talking about self-knowledge here discussed assumes that the most pervasive false construction of the self is an ego around whose specific satisfactions the world is to be structured. Hence: first, this analysis is empty if it is not a tool for the questioning, by the disadvantaged as well as by the powerful themselves, of illusory (and thus oppressive) constructions of the world; secondly, if liberation is not to be a mere reversal of the master–slave relationship, it must recognise what it is in human self-perception that generates and entrenches illusion and slavery, and thirdly, liberation as overthrowing the bondage of the other's (oppressive) desire remains determined by that desire so long as it remains primarily negative and does not move on to address the question of how we might *now* imagine shared satisfactions. In other words, victimage is a dangerous rhetorical instrument, if it means that a language of primitive innocence violated is allowed to distract attention from the vulnerability of all historical schemes of self-presentation, particular and corporate, to the seductions of self-finalising, closure to criticism.

The recovery of an oppressed, victimised history is a profoundly necessary moment in so many enterprises of self-knowing – whether black history, workers' history in Britain, or the individual and terrible histories of abused children. Isolated from any energy in asking how present reciprocities might be turned towards shared goods, how desire becomes more than desire for the end of the oppressor's desire, the language of the victim can become sterile and collusive. The personal is not the political if it stops at being a programme of negation and the reinstatement of an injured ego; and the political remains tribal if dominated by *ressentiment*. In establishing this, the project of a self-knowledge that emphasises contingency and the non-finality of our 'constructions' of selfhood may have its place, even when all allowances have been made for the danger of this language in its turn.

Two concluding reflections. The first has to do with the more strictly philosophical import of all this – and, less directly, with the popular contemporary rhetoric of self-discovery. If we were to ask, 'How might we "test" for self-knowledge in ourselves or others?' it looks as if the answer might lie in trying to deal with questions like, 'Is there a pattern of behaviour here suggesting an unwillingness to learn or to be enlarged?' or 'Is there an obsessive quality to acts of self-presentation (in speech especially) that would indicate a fixed and defended image of needs that must be met for this self to sustain its position or power?' or 'Is there a refusal to deal verbally or imaginatively with the limits of power – ultimately with mortality?' In other words, we do not look first for acquaintance with any particular vocabulary of 'self-analysis' (we don't test for *information*). This may be a rather banal observation, so philosophically obvious as not to need saying; but in a culture where self-help books about self-knowledge, not least of a religious tinge, abound, we may well need reminding that a person may be possessed of a fluent vocabulary, well able to plot him- or herself on the charts of temperament and *attrait* and to retell their biography in the idiom of fashionable psychobabble; and yet continue to act in a way that seems to deny the recognition of mortality and the necessary ironies that go with it. And in so far as the present vogue for a religious rhetoric of self-awareness relies heavily on this kind of technology of re-description, it is indeed at odds with what the Christian spiritual tradition (and others) has meant by self-knowing. This is, of course, perfectly compatible with saying that, when we recognise a crisis of truthfulness, the power of our habitual self-deceits, there is a place for theories of trauma, repression, the characteristic patterns of personality type or whatever, in unblocking certain channels and diagnosing the scale of our defensiveness; all this (a good servant and a bad master) has its role in becoming reacquainted with our contingency, even if it cannot deliver everything. The religious believer and the analytical or therapeutic theorist, however, will have different things to say about what more than theory is required.

And last, *when* is the injunction, 'Know thyself' likely to be uttered, and *who* has the authority to utter it? When it can be shown that my actions are at odds with what might be expected of an agent both reasoning and mortal. When King Lear's daughters agree, 'He hath ever but slenderly known himself', they are pointing to the tension which his behaviour exhibits between verbal recognition of mortality and the obsessive clinging to the image of a royal self. Yet their own frightening egotisms disqualify them from having the right to execute judgement on his self-deceit. His eyes are opened in two ways: by the naked madman on the heath and by Cordelia; by Poor Tom to mortality and impotence, by Cordelia to the need of love. Who or what can command us to know ourselves? The dispossessed life – whether Tom's utter lack of standing and pride (itself in the play, of course, a *strategy* of dispossession on the part of Edgar), Cordelia's abnegation of revenge ('No cause, no cause!').[28] The injunction is there for us in the way in which the holy life interrupts our habitual constructions (an echo of Kierkegaard's *Philosophical Fragments* here)[29] by making for me in the world the room I thought I had to conquer and possess.

NOTES

Chapter 3 The Bible Today: Reading & Hearing

1 Alan Jacobs, *A Theology of Reading: The Hermeneutics of Love*. Boulder, Colorado: Westview Press, 2001, 107–12.
2 See especially his collection of *Essays on Biblical Interpretation*. London: SPCK, 1981.
3 Peter Ochs, 'Scripture', 104–18 in ed. Ford, David, Quash, Ben and Soskice, Janet Martin, *Fields of Faith: Theology and Religious Studies for the Twenty-First Century*. Cambridge: Cambridge University Press, 2005, 111.
4 Ibid.
5 Ibid., 113.
6 Vanhoozer, Kevin J., *The Drama of Doctrine: A Canonical Linguistic Approach to Christian Theology*. Louisville, Kentucky: Westminster John Knox Press, 2005, 137.
7 See, for example, the 'Preface to the third edition' of his commentary on *The Epistle to the Romans*, tr. Hoskyns, Edwin Clement. Oxford: Oxford University Press, 1933, 15–20.

Chapter 4 God's Workshop

1 References to the Rule are to the English translation (ed. Fry, Timothy OSB). Collegeville, Minnesota: Liturgical Press, 1982.
2 ed. Barton, Stephen, *Holiness, Past and Present*. London/New York: T. & T. Clark, 2003, 261.
3 Nicholl, Donald, *The Testing of Hearts: A Pilgrim's Journal*. London: Darton, Longman and Todd, 1989.
4 Ibid., 62.

5 Ibid., 142.
6 Ibid., 143.
7 Needleman, Jacob, *Lost Christianity*. New York: Doubleday, 1980, especially 117–19 and chapter 8, *passim*.
8 Nicholl, op. cit., 224.
9 Coventry, John, Weakland, Rembert and others, *Religious Life Today*. Tenbury Wells: Fowler Wright Books, 1971, 44.

CHAPTER 5 URBAN SPIRITUALITY

1 Wells, Sam, *Community-Led Regeneration and the Local Church*. Cambridge: Grove Booklets, 2003.
2 Shanks, Andrew, *God and Modernity*. London: Routledge, 2000, 29–33.

CHAPTER 7 CONTEMPLATION AND MISSION

1 de Lubac, Henri, *Paradoxes of Faith*. San Francisco: Ignatius Press, 2000, 69.
2 Merton, Thomas, *Elected Silence* (the British revised version of *The Seven Storey Mountain*). London: Hollis and Carter, 1949, 303.
3 See above, n.7 to Chapter 4.
4 Lubich, Chiara, ed. Vandeleene, Michel, *Essential Writings: Spirituality, Dialogue, Culture*. London: New City, 2007, 37.
5 de Lubac, op. cit., 111–12.
6 Ibid., 114.

CHAPTER 8 ICONS AND THE PRACTICE OF PRAYER

1 Nes, Solrunn, *The Uncreated Light: An Iconographical Study of the Transfiguration in the Eastern Church*. Grand Rapids, Michigan: Eerdmans, 2007, 74–84, especially 77 and 81.
2 Nes, op. cit., has a fine account of this aspect of Feofan's style against the background of the controversies involving St Gregory Palamas (105–70); see also plate 13 in her book.

3 Ouspensky, Leonid and Lossky, Vladimir, *The Meaning of Icons*. Crestwood, NY: St Vladimir's Seminary Press, 1982, 39–40.

4 Ibid., 40–1.

5 See Maximus, *Third Century on Love*, 40, in *The Philokalia*, Volume 2, tr. Palmer, G. E. H., Sherrard, Philip and Ware, Kallistos. London: Faber & Faber, 1981, 89.

6 In his treatise *On Spiritual Knowledge*, 89, in *The Philokalia*, Volume 1, tr. Palmer, G. E. H., Sherrard, Philip and Ware, Kallistos. London: Faber & Faber, 1979, 288.

CHAPTER 10 TERESA AND THE SCRIPTURES

1 References to Teresa's writings are to the translations by Kieran Kavanaugh and Otilio Rodriguez, published by the Institute of Carmelite Studies in Washington, three volumes, 1976, 1989 and 1985. All contain scriptural indices, though these need to be used carefully as, for example, they sometimes ascribe a citation or allusion as being to St Mark's Gospel, where it is much more likely that Teresa is using a Matthean parallel (see below).

2 See the excellent treatment in Ahlgren, Gillian, *Teresa of Avila and the Politics of Sanctity*, Ithaca and London: Cornell University Press, 1996, especially chapter 4; see also Williams, Rowan, *Teresa of Avila*, London and New York: Continuum, 1991, chapters 1 and 4.

3 On the role of religious houses in civic life, see Bilinkoff, Jodi, *The Avila of St Teresa*, Ithaca and London: Cornell University Press, 1989. See also, more recently, Perez, Joseph, *Teresa de Avila y la España de su tiempo*, Madrid: Algaba, 2007.

4 See especially Ahlgren, op. cit., 86–97.

5 The new Tridentine liturgy of 1570 finally established the use of the Song of Songs as the first reading for the Mass on St Mary Magdalene's feast, replacing the widespread mediaeval use of Proverbs 31. It is not clear whether the new usage was current in Spain before the completion of

the Tridentine reform, and if so whether the Carmelite rite was affected. Boyce, James, *Carmelite Liturgy and Spiritual Identity: The Choir Books of Krakow*, Turnhout: Brepols, 2008, contains much useful information on the mediaeval Carmelite liturgy including (33 ff.) the antiphons for the feast of St Mary Magdalene: one of these (*Dum esset Rex*) is drawn from the Song of Songs (1.12), but this is not unique (as far as I know) to Carmelite usage.

6   de Certeau, Michel, *The Mystic Fable*: Volume One, *The Sixteenth and Seventeenth Centuries*. Chicago and London: Chicago University Press, 1992, 188–200, discusses Teresa's rhetoric as seeking an answer to the question, 'Who am I?' within a 'Catholic space' that has become fractured and problematic.

CHAPTER 11   TERESA AND THE EUCHARIST

1   Peers, E. Allison, *Mother of Carmel: A Portrait of St Teresa of Jesus*. London: SCM Press, 1961.

2   Dicken, E. W. Trueman, *The Crucible of Love: A Study of the Mysticism of St Teresa of Jesus and St John of the Cross*. London: Darton, Longman and Todd, 1963.

3   References and citations from the translation by Kieran Kavanaugh and Otilio Rodriguez, published by the Institute of Carmelite Studies, Washington DC, 1980.

4   The first major attacks by French Protestants on images and furnishings in churches occurred in 1560, as Teresa and her associates were beginning to discuss concrete plans for a new style of monastic life.

5   Ed. cit., 47.

6   Ibid., 51.

7   Ibid., 167.

8   Ibid.

9   Compare her *Meditations on the Song of Songs*, 4.8, on Christ looking after what is mine as I look after what is his. 4.10 incidentally alludes, in very much the same terms as the *Way* text, to Christ's 'remaining' in the sacrament.

10   *Way of Perfection* 167–8.

11   Ibid., 169.

12   Ibid., 172.

13   Ibid., 168.

14   Ibid.

15   Ibid., 169.

16   Augustine, *de trinitate* IV.xx.28–9, especially xx.29: *sicut enim natum esse est filio* a patre *esse, ita mitti est filio cognosci quod ab illo sit.*

17   Translated by Howard V. Hong and Edna H. Hong, Princeton: Princeton University Press, 1985; see especially chapter IV, 55–71: 'knowing a historical fact ... by no means makes the eyewitness a follower' (59).

18   *Way of Perfection* 34.8, 172.

19   Ibid., 172.

20   Ibid., 173.

21   No. 52 of the *Spiritual Testimonies*, 346, in volume I of the Institute of Carmelite Studies translation, Washington DC, 1976.

22   See the classical statement of the one coming of Christ to the Father in time and eternity in Dix, Gregory, *The Shape of the Liturgy*. London: A. & C. Black, 1945, 262–3, 265–6: 'the eucharist is nothing else but the gesture of the Son of Man towards His Father as He passes into the Kingdom of God. (266). I doubt whether Dix would have known the Teresian passage, but it would have added a further confirmatory dimension to his own synthesis.

23   See especially 9.4 on her sense of calling to stay with Christ in Gethsemane.

24   *Way of Perfection* 35.5, 176.

Chapter 12   Julian of Norwich's Way

1   Turner, Denys, *Julian of Norwich, Theologian*. New Haven and London: Yale University Press, 2011.

2   For the main points, see especially Gillespie and Ross, 'The Apophatic Image: The Poetics of Effacement in Julian of

Norwich', *The Mediaeval Mystical Tradition in England V.* Cambridge: D. S. Brewer, 1992, 53–7.

3   I refer for convenience to ed. Watson, Nicholas and Jenkins, Jacqueline, *The Writings of Julian of Norwich*. University Park, Pennsylvania: University of Pennsylvania Press, 2006. This is a hybrid text, combining readings from the Sloane, Paris and Westminster manuscripts (see 35–40); not an uncontroversial method. For a critical text based on S1 (the first of the Sloane manuscripts), which has a good claim to be more faithful to the original diction, see ed. Glasscoe, Marion, *Julian of Norwich: A Revelation of Divine Love*, Exeter Mediaeval English Texts and Studies. Exeter: University of Exeter, 1986 (second edition).

4   Watson and Jenkins, op. cit., 194.

5   Irenaeus of Lyons, *Adversus haereses* IV.34.

6   'Poetry as "Menace" and "Atonement"', in Hill, Geoffrey, *Collected Critical Essays*. Oxford: Oxford University Press, 2008, 3–20; quotation from 19.

7   Ibid., 4.

8   *The Works of St John of the Cross*, volume II, tr. Peers, E. Allison. London: Burns & Oates, 1934, 455–65, especially 458–9.

9   Turner, op. cit., chapter 2, which explains with exemplary clarity the presumed relation in Julian's writing between divine gift and human freedom and defends Julian against the charge of 'quietism'.

10   Ibid., 33, 60–5.

11   'Necessity' is the wrong word here, as there is no question of any specific sinful act being predetermined by the divine will for the human will to perform; see, once again, Turner, op. cit., 38–46.

12   In the introduction to his Penguin translation of *Revelations of Divine Love*. Harmondsworth: Penguin Books, 1966, 38.

13   London: Darton, Longman and Todd, 1977.

14   Op. cit., 47.

15   Ibid., 63–72.

16 Ibid., 48.

17 Augustine, *de doctrina Christiana* I.iii, xxxi ff.

Chapter 13 'Know Thyself': What Kind of an Injunction?

1 Laing, R. D., *The Divided Self*. London: Tavistock Publications, 1960.

2 Ibid., 87–8.

3 I rely chiefly on Lacan's *The Language of the Self: The Function of Language in Psychoanalysis*, translated with notes and commentary by Anthony Wilden. Baltimore: Johns Hopkins University Press, 1968.

4 Ibid., 11, 31, 62–3, 83–5.

5 Ferry, L. and Renaut, A., *French Philosophy of the '60's: An Essay on Antihumanism*. Amherst: University of Massachusetts Press, 1990, chapter 6. Their treatment more or less ignores the Lacanian emphasis on the analyst as catalyst of proper intersubjectivity, though it does identify elements of primitivist romantic pathos in some of Lacan's discussions (197, 203).

6 Lacan, op. cit., 84–5.

7 Girard, R., *Things Hidden Since the Foundation of the World*. London: Athlone Press, 1987, 403–5. 'Lacan falls into the error that is shared by the whole psychoanalytic school when he writes about capture by the imaginary – a desire that is not inscribed within the system of cultural differences and so could not be a desire for difference, but necessarily bears on something like the same, the identical, the image of one's ego, etc.' (404). The point is a crucial one: the Lacanian view of the subject as directed towards death is only intelligible if there is indeed some kind of reality prior to being spoken to, being engaged with, even if this is conceived only as a notional or regulative level of the psyche's life. Even in such a minimal form, it affirms a priority of sameness over difference and nature over culture, which it is Girard's aim (in his own terms) to demythologise.

8 I have in mind especially the varieties of popularised Jungianism now vastly influential in books and courses on spiritual direction – the Myers–Briggs personality typology, the categories of the 'Enneagram', and so forth. These techniques of analysis have great practical usefulness, as many experienced spiritual directors confirm; but presented in terms of theory, they have some very questionable elements, not least in the language sometimes explicitly used of a 'purity of essence' preceding socialisation, and in the mechanical and fixed ways in which personality types are sometimes presented in the self-help books generated by the popularity of this style of interpretation.

9 ed. Robinson, J., *The Nag Hammadi Library*. Leiden: E. J. Brill, 1977, 99–116.

10 Ibid., 109–10.

11 Ibid., 37–49.

12 Ibid., 118–30.

13 Ibid., 18.

14 Ibid., 123.

15 Ibid., 130.

16 According to classical sources, it was inscribed at the door of the shrine of Apollo's oracle at Delphi.

17 Robinson, op. cit., 122.

18 Ibid., 124, 127.

19 Ibid., 121.

20 Augustine in *Confessions* VII.2 summarises the argument of his friend Nebridius about the difficulties of a thoroughgoing dualist metaphysic: either God is vulnerable to change and chance – in which case, it is perfectly conceivable that good will be defeated in the universe, and that therefore the good is not identical with the real; or God and the good are not vulnerable, in which case there is no need for a properly dualist theory in the first place. Divine self-alienation and primordial conflict between equipollent powers are equally insupportable positions in any intelligible metaphysic.

21 Translated by Kilian Walsh, OCSO, in the *Cistercian Fathers* series. Kalamazoo: Cistercian Publications, 1971 and 1976.

22 Cf. Williams, Rowan, *Resurrection: Interpreting the Easter Gospel*. London: Darton, Longman and Todd, 1982, 29: 'The self *is* ... what the past is doing now.' This formulation was criticised as fanciful and imprecise, but I should still want to defend it in so far as it represents the sense to which Augustine witnesses that present 'selfhood' is not an arena of open choices confronting an abstractly free volition, but a territory marked out by preceding determinations (by self and others), which mould, in ways frequently inaccessible to us, what can be and is done.

23 I have attempted a slightly more extended discussion in 'The Paradoxes of Self-Knowledge in Augustine's Trinitarian Thought', Williams, Rowan, *On Augustine*, London: Bloomsbury, 2016, 155–70.

24 Ibid.; for a perspective on the Wittgensteinian approach to self-knowledge, there is a useful article by Godfrey Vesey, 'Self-Aquaintance and the Meaning of "I"', in *Inner and Outer: Essays on a Philosophical Myth*. London: Macmillan, 1991.

25 See the celebrated section in Gregory of Nyssa's *contra Eunomium* II. 107ff. (Migne, *Patrologia Graeca* 45,945 Dff.; in the more recent edition of Jaeger, which corrects the numbering of the books in Migne, vol. I, 258ff.) on our inability to give an account of what our own souls actually are in any finished way – a point designed to reinforce Gregory's insistence that the knowledge of God, in whose image the soul is made, is similarly unfinishable, eternally open or expanding.

26 'Unlimited' time not, of course, in the sense that Augustine did not believe in human mortality or the end of the world at a determinate point; but in the sense that no term is fixed to the work of individual or society in the attainment of the good *within* history. We could never claim to have reached a plateau, nor is the failure to realise the fullness of God's justice within history an irreparable or unforgivable delinquency. All human achievement is provisional, all is therefore capable of flux for better or worse; there is, from *our* point of view in history, 'always' a future.

27 Girard, op. cit., Bk II, Bk III, ch. 1.
28 On Lear as a text about knowledge and self-knowledge, about the knowledge we need and the knowledge (of mastery, of information) that must be foregone in the process of moral maturation, even salvation, see the brilliant essay of Stanley Cavell, 'The Avoidance of Love: A Reading of *King Lear*', in *Must We Mean What We Say?* Cambridge: Cambridge University Press, 1976, 267–353. My debt to this and other works of Cavell will be evident.
29 *Philosophical Fragments/Johannes Climacus*, ed. and trans. Hong, Howard V. and Hong, Edna H., Princeton: Princeton University Press, 1985, Part II, esp. 30–5, and Part III, 39–46.

ACKNOWLEDGEMENTS

Chapter 1: originally published in *Sobornost* 7.5, 1977, 401–3.

Chapter 2: edited transcript of the Hildegard Lecture delivered at Holy Rood House, Thirsk, 7 February 2003.

Chapter 3: the Larkin-Stuart Lecture, delivered at Trinity College, Toronto, 16 April 2007.

Chapter 4: delivered at Trinity Church, Wall Street, New York, 29 April 2003.

Chapter 5: originally published in Walker, Andrew, ed., *Spirituality in the City,* London: SPCK 2005, 15–26.

Chapter 6: originally published in Percy, Martyn, ed., *Intimate Affairs: Sexuality and Spirituality in Perspective*, London: Darton, Longman and Todd, 1997, 21–31.

Chapter 7: delivered in Rome to the Synod of Bishops of the Roman Catholic Church, 10 October 2012.

Chapter 8: edited transcript of a lecture delivered at the Royal Academy of Arts, 16 January 2009.

Chapter 9: originally published in *Mount Carmel: A Quarterly Review of the Spiritual Life*, 2015.

Chapter 10: delivered at a conference on Teresa of Avila at the University of Oxford, 28 March 2015; due to appear in the proceedings of the conference, edited by Colin Thompson.

Chapter 11: originally published in *Teresa de Jesus: Patrimonio de la humanidad. Actas del Congreso Mundial Teresiano en el Centenario de su nacimiento (1515–2015)*. Burgos: Monte Carmelo-Universidad de la Mistica, 2016, vol. 1, 519–30; also in the forthcoming proceedings of a conference at St Mary's University, Twickenham, June 2015, edited by Peter Tyler.

Chapter 12: the Julian Lecture delivered at the Julian Shrine, Norwich, 12 May 2014; published as a pamphlet by the Shrine.

Chapter 13; originally published in McGhee, Michael, ed., *Philosophy, Religion and the Spiritual Life* (Royal Institute of Philosophy Supplement 32). Cambridge: Cambridge University Press, 1992, 211–27.

(Minor alterations to some previously published texts have been incorporated for clarification or to remove outdated references.)

ABOUT THE AUTHOR

Rowan Williams was Professor of Divinity at Oxford University before becoming Bishop of Monmouth in 1992. After ten years as Archbishop of Canterbury, he became Master of Magdalene College, Cambridge in 2013, and is internationally well-known as a theologian, poet and commentator on current affairs. He is also a regular contributor to the *New Statesman*. Rowan Williams's recent books include *On Augustine* and *The Edge of Words*, both published by Bloomsbury Continuum.

A NOTE ON THE TYPE

The text of this book is set in Linotype Sabon, a typeface named after the type founder, Jacques Sabon. It was designed by Jan Tschichold and jointly developed by Linotype, Monotype and Stempel in response to a need for a typeface to be available in identical form for mechanical hot metal composition and hand composition using foundry type.

Tschichold based his design for Sabon roman on a font engraved by Garamond, and Sabon italic on a font by Granjon. It was first used in 1966 and has proved an enduring modern classic.